BlunderBoss

BLUNDERBOSS

How Britain's Bosses are Failing You

Roger Trapp

CAPSTONE

First published 1999 by
Capstone US
Business Books Network
163 Central Avenue
Suite 2
Hopkins Professional Building
Dover
NH 03820
USA

Capstone Publishing Limited
Oxford Centre for Innovation
Mill Street
Oxford OX2 0JX
United Kingdom
http://www.capstone.co.uk

British Library Cataloguing in Publication Data
A CIP catalogue record for this book is available from the British Library

ISBN 1-900961-64-4

Typeset in 11/15 pt Sabon by
Sparks Computer Solutions, Oxford
http://www.sparks.co.uk
Printed and bound by
T.J. International Ltd, Padstow, Cornwall

This book is printed on acid-free paper

Substantial discounts on bulk quantities of Capstone books are available to corporations, professional associations and other organizations. For details telephone Capstone Publishing on (+44-1865-798623) or fax (+44-1865-240941).

DEDICATION

For Deirdre

CONTENTS

WHY THIS BOOK?

This is a book born of anger, frustration and, above all, puzzlement.

Received wisdom has it that today's top business executives are more highly skilled, harder working and generally more impressive than all their predecessors. And yet in a dozen years as a business journalist I have been struck by just how few seem to measure up to these standards.

It is no accident that there is only a small core of business leaders deemed truly inspirational. The computer kings Bill Gates and Andrew Grove (former chief executive of Intel, the other half of the 'Wintel sandwich') and Jack Welch of General Electric of the USA are sometimes joined by Britain's own Richard Branson. But the list does not go much further.

Nevertheless, chief executives of all sorts of companies are – particularly when claiming hefty hikes in pay – forever protesting their clout. Though UK companies tend not to figure very high in tables of international rankings on turnover, profitability or investment in research and development, and British companies have often made a hash of expanding overseas, we are assured that the best of British can stand comparison with the best in the world.

No doubt, it is such a claim that makes them so alluring to the politicians – especially those of a New Labour hue – who call on them to help sort out weighty national problems. Never mind that the organisations they run are often in such poor shape that it is hard to see what wisdom they have to impart. And never mind that the downsizing, cost-cutting and other tough tactics practised by many of these companies actually contribute to these problems.

But those of us who – unlike the Westminster cheerleaders – have actually worked in these large companies, and the professional firms and public-sector organisations that so often ape them, know better.

From my own experience, I can say that media companies might be full of what are now termed 'knowledge workers', but that does not mean that they have always been enthusiastic converts from the old command-and-control ways of doing things. One organisation for which I worked saw giving editors of a certain rank keys to the executive lavatories as a valuable perk, while it is a well-known truism that there is nothing like a communications organisation to forget about communicating with its staff.

In addition, of course, when union power was at its height, it was the people running newspapers – just as much as those at the head of the car industry – who apparently lost the will to manage or to take the tough decisions that being in business often demands. Though he hardly fits most people's idea of a business hero, Rupert Murdoch deserves some credit for demonstrating how the newspaper industry could be saved from itself.

But at least these companies tend to allow a little dissent. In many other workplaces the sense of fear is so persuasive that a heads-down mentality reigns.

The result is that people throughout organisations – whether they be international retailers, teaching hospitals or firms of accountants – are so intent on not doing the wrong thing that they do very little that adds value, to use today's jargon. Management consultants and their clients talk a lot about the extent to which business processes have changed, but the reality is that they are not that different from how they were decades ago. Much time is still wasted filling out forms and obeying protocols in the mistaken belief that this aids efficiency. People in business are busier than they used to be because they tend to be fewer in number than before and because of the greater emphasis placed on speed. But they are not necessarily more productive in the true sense of coming up with something worthwhile.

The problem, as the US academic Warren Bennis has pointed out, is that there is too much emphasis on management and not enough on leadership. America and its business community, he says in his book *Managing People is like Herding Cats*, has been managed to the brink of ruin. But the same is true of Britain – if not more so, because of the antipathy to risk taking that seems to pervade the culture.

It is this mismatch between British business's claims and its actual achievements that is the cause of all that anger, frustration and puzzlement.

The anger stems from the sense of what might have been. Companies as varied as Hewlett-Packard and Body Shop show that business has tremendous scope for providing people with a worthwhile way of spending their days. But in too many others the cynical pursuit of the short-term advantage wins out.

The frustration is a result of the fact that this obviously does not have to be the case. Business people in Britain are as likely as their American cousins to think that because what they sell is complicated then business must be complex. But those in organisations that have enjoyed long-term success tend to stress simplicity and the basics.

The puzzlement is simply an inability to understand why we have put up with all this nonsense for so long. It is widely acknowledged that commonsense dictates that treating people fairly, giving them a sense of purpose, appealing to their values are not just likely to produce a happy workplace. They are also likely to produce a successful one. And yet so few organisations do any of these things. No wonder that one chief executive has ventured the view that commonsense is a misnomer since it is obviously so rare. And, he might have added, nowhere more so than in business.

ACKNOWLEDGEMENTS

This book would not have been possible without the help and support of numerous people.

Over the years, too many consultants, academics and business executives to name have spared me a great deal of their time and – wittingly or otherwise – contributed to the thinking displayed here.

In addition, I am grateful to Jeremy Warner, business and City editor of the Independent, and other colleagues - past and present - for encouraging me to delve into a field that has become increasingly fascinating and of importance to us all.

Mark Allin and Richard Burton of Capstone were also hugely helpful in focusing my ideas.

But special thanks go to my wife, Deirdre, and three young daughters, who have put up with countless extra hours at my desk and a general distractedness while this project has been brought to fruition.

Finally, apologies to REM and Dan Penn and Chips Moman for borrowing the titles to Chapters 1 and 6 from their songs.

THE PROBLEM
AND ITS CAUSES

The average member of the British public could be forgiven for thinking that when it comes to the country's business performance the past two decades have been a waste of time.

Margaret Thatcher's 'economic miracle', defeat of the unions and hundreds of 'bonfires of red tape' appear to have produced little discernible benefit. Companies are certainly more comfortable with modern business jargon than they were, so we are constantly told that their processes have been re-engineered, their operations restructured and their people focused on core competencies. But what all this hides is that – in large part – they are still as badly run, still as apparently powerless to deal with the vicissitudes of life and still as demoralising to work in as they always were.

Industries which we are supposed to be good at – such as banking and music – are now largely in overseas hands, while in hard-core sectors – such as engineering and automobile manufacture – the picture is even bleaker. Barclays pulled out of investing banking and, casting about for other ways to keep the shareholders happy, lost its thrusting chief executive. EMI, shorn of the Thorn part in a demerger designed to 'enhance value', became a subject of constant takeover speculation. BTR, once the proud owner of Slazenger and other brands, sold off its best bits before, running into the embrace of Siebe in late 1998, arguably the one British engineering company to have made a go of it in recent years – albeit partly under the direction of Americans. Rover, having supposedly been sorted out by Sir Michael Edwardes, Sir Graham Day and George (now Lord) Simpson, found itself at the centre of the debate over the 'productivity gap' between Britain and the rest of the world. At the end of 1998, it was estimated that there was a 30 per cent differential between its workers and the German equivalents of the latest owner, BMW. No doubt, given that the McKinsey & Co. report on productivity that informed so much of Chancellor Gordon Brown's 1998 pre-Budget statement reckoned that Britain was generally about 40 per cent behind its supposed competitors, some would say that Rover was doing quite well.

But that is the point. British business, for all its pretensions to play on the world stage, seems content to bumble along. The lack of urgency, the sloppiness about time-keeping and disregard for service in general, with which we are all familiar from our dealings with builders, various utilities and train companies, are pervasive throughout all sectors of industry. Retailers complain about sluggish sales but seem unconcerned about their inability to supply what people want, exporters claim that they have brilliant products but cannot attract buyers because the strong pound makes them unattractive and manufacturers seem intent on making what they want rather than what the market demands. It is not just this writer who is angry, frustrated and puzzled. Those sentiments are shared by just about everybody who is touched by business – and, with the growing commercialisation of the public sector, that means us all.

In this egocentric age, we are encouraged to think that we are always treading new ground. In terms of business, this means that, though companies have never been bigger nor made greater profits, they have seldom been harder places in which to work.

Leaving aside the fact that these days, thanks largely to technology, many fewer people than before have to risk life and limb in the name of business, it is often argued that the downsizing, the increasing pace of change, the longer hours, the lack of job security and the rest of it make working an increasingly tough proposition.

That may be. But business has been under the cosh for years. In the expansionist years immediately after World War II and in the 'never had it so good' days of the early 1960s, books came out questioning the corporation in much the same way as we do now. And half a century ago, W.H. Auden started his poem 'The Managers' with the lines:

> 'In the bad old days it was not so bad:
> The top of the ladder
> Was an amusing place to sit; success
> Meant quite a lot – leisure
> And huge meals, more palaces filled with more
> Objects, books, girls, horses
> Than one would ever get around to.'

But though our dissatisfaction with the way things are is probably unoriginal, there does seem to be a difference this time around because there are indications that things do not have to be like this. Developments on the fringes of business, while encouraging some, are creating frustrations in others.

This is why, although on the face of it business is enjoying something of a golden era, there is such a widespread feeling of unease. In the main, those that have emerged from the deep recession of the early 1990s look to be in good shape; they are lean and mean and in expansive mood. And yet something seems to be wrong. It all looks very shaky. One day boom, the next profit warnings and restructurings.

This intangible something is making its presence felt in the growing doubts about whether the much talked-about battle against inflation and the boom–bust cycle is really over.

In Britain, this anxiety was given a solid basis in the autumn of 1998 by two separate but nevertheless linked events. The first was the report by the management consultancy McKinsey & Co referred to above that apparently gave the lie to all the stories about the marked improvement in Britain's industrial performance over the previous two decades; it showed a 40 per cent 'productivity gap' between the UK and other industrialised countries.

Commentators have since debated long and hard definitions of productivity. But the damage had been done.

Then, Marks & Spencer – for years, by common consent, Britain's most admired company – reported a sharp downturn in profits and then descended into a good old-fashioned boardroom row over who should succeed Sir Richard Greenbury as chief executive. Forget for a moment that even before the figures were out certain commentators were starting to suggest that the company's 'offering' was looking dated by comparison with those in other high street stores. And leave aside the notion that institutional investors were only going to accept one person being both chairman and chief executive long after such a combination of roles had ceased to be fashionable, so long as the company kept performing. The incident created a sense that, if this could happen to 'Marks and Sparks', nobody was safe.

Such episodes only reinforce the British suspicion of success. Give or take the odd financial crisis or other setback, the USA seems as vibrant as ever – continually throwing up new companies in all kinds of sectors, many of them trying out new business models. But in Britain it is different. Tony Blair's New Labour may have thrown tradition to the wall by seeing business's potential for helping to deal with certain social problems. However, the suspicion of business remains.

Beneath the surface, it is clear that there is widespread dissatisfaction with how business, in the main, operates. Nor is this just a view held by trade unionists and other traditional business bashers. In fact, it is more likely to be voiced by the legions of people – often long-serving middle managers – 'let go' in the early years of this decade as large companies in the USA and Britain used the recession as a smokescreen for starting the large-scale restructurings, consolidations and downsizings that – whatever the rhetoric – are still going on today.

Words such as 'trust', 'loyalty' and 'commitment' now pepper the management consultants' lexicons. But it is precisely the perceived lack of such qualities among the highly paid captains of industry that is causing such a groundswell of ill feeling.

Though such people are supposedly so well remunerated largely because of their intelligence, vision, insight and the rest, they seem to struggle with the notion that living under an almost constant shadow of redundancy does not exactly create a feeling of well-being, let alone encourage the risk taking upon which growth and innovation – the latest buzzwords – depend. And for all the positive messages put out by gurus and consultants who are often already living the free-agent life, many do not find the prospect of being knowledge workers for hire to the highest bidders more alluring than a career working through the ranks with the same employer.

If these 'leaders' cannot inspire the people who work for them, they certainly have a job with most of the population. Thirty years after the first business schools opened in the country, Britain is still rather suspicious about those who actually work in business, as Jeremy Warner, business and City editor of the *Independent*, said in a commentary in February 1998 in the wake of a spate of bad publicity for Richard Branson.

Pointing out that there is still 'a tendency in Britain to mistrust business success, even when it comes from someone as apparently user-friendly as Mr Branson', he wrote: 'For all Mrs Thatcher's efforts, she failed to shift this anti-business undercurrent in British culture. The fact that Mr Branson has done so much himself to change perceptions, and make entrepreneurialism something British people aspire to once more, is in itself an admirable thing.'

Similarly, when later the same year, the hugely successful US investment bank Goldman Sachs opted to abandon its private partnership status in favour of becoming a publicly owned company with a flotation value put at about $35 billion (until the financial turmoil of 1998 caused a change of mind), there was a large amount of media comment. Much of this was outside the business pages – presumably on the grounds that the fortunes former partners in the firm would make were yet another example of City fat cattery.

As Warner said in another column, of 20 June 1998, the fact that UK coverage of the Goldmans move far outweighed that in the USA 'tells you a lot about the continuing cultural differences between the US and the UK. Despite the Thatcher reforms of the 1980s, we are still generally suspicious and jealous of uninherited wealth, unless it is made by sports and rock stars, which seems to make it somehow alright.'

It is apparently acceptable to advise businesses as a lawyer or an accountant, but to be 'in business' as such is still not quite right. Significantly, perhaps, it is on this issue that Britain's New Labour most resembles Old Labour; any substantial gains not achieved either through the National Lottery or through participating in one of the 'Cool Britannia' industries, such as pop music, fashion or design, seem suspect to large ranks of the party. This explains the open hostility meted out to members of the business community from parliamentary committees and also the repeated – if somewhat doomed – efforts of various ministers to stress how they are not anti-business. So much for the desire to create an entrepreneurial environment to rival that of California.

Such organisations as the Royal Society for the Encouragement of Arts, Manufactures and Commerce and the Design Council are making attempts to change such attitudes with various initiatives aimed at alerting school and college leavers and those still involved in education to the rich opportunities available in the business world. But, though well-intentioned, such efforts are almost bound to have little impact on their own.

Just telling people, or even – thanks to the wonders of modern technology – showing them with the aid of vivid images, is unlikely to win over the unconverted. After all, young people do not want to become pop stars or sports heroes because they were introduced to such people via school (in fact, such moves would be likely to have the opposite effect); they aspire to such careers partly because of the lifestyle opportunities that they bring, but mostly because they think lives led in that way might be fun.

So could it be that, even after all these years of companies talking about getting leaner, fitter and flatter, the feeling is that a life in business entails, at worst, either constantly being on the receiving end of or meting out redundancies and plant closures or, at best, endless politicking in an attempt to steer a way through the bureaucratic maze? After all, if cartoonists such as Dilbert creator Scott Adams and columnists such as *Fortune's* Stanley Bing portray it that way, it really must be true, mustn't it?

As John Case writes in his book *The Open-Book Management Experience*, the people in companies 'aren't doing so well. They are anxious and frustrated. They regard their employers with a baleful mixture of mistrust and misgiving. Above all, they are deeply cynical.' Quoting from an article by TJ and Sandar Larkin in the May–June 1996 issue of the *Harvard Business Review* that said that the frontline workforce had become cynical through and through rather than just sprinkled with cynics, he adds: 'The icon of our age isn't the Organisation Man, it's Dilbert and his pals.'

Certain that life as 'a corporate gook' is a long way off being fun, the best and the brightest in the world's leading industrial nations are apt to make a beeline for just about any career rather than one in what is traditionally termed business, or commerce. Namely, the sort of organisations that either are or aspire to be formidable presences around the world in such fields as consumer goods, food, industrial components, transport and the like.

The sad fact is, of course, that even though bright young graduates all around the world avoid going into business in their droves, they do not succeed in staying away from it entirely. So convinced of the wisdom of business techniques are politicians, public sector administrators and those running the professional firms and other workplaces that young people opt to join instead, that they find it almost impossible to resist introducing the latest fads to their own organisations – even though they are often at just that time proving to be fundamentally flawed.

In short, though some are recognising business's capacity to play a fuller part in society and others are realising that in many areas it – and individual players – are already more powerful than many national governments would care to imagine, there is more than a lingering scent of cynicism. Even some of those organisations that appear to be genuinely trying to be different are looked upon with suspicion on the grounds that companies and their advisers are apt to appropriate such concepts as 'values' and 'integrity' for marketing purposes rather than demonstrating that they represent deep-rooted beliefs.

But does it have to be that way? This book will argue not. It will suggest that a 'we'll focus on the profits and get what we can while we can' approach is not the only workable business model. Indeed, it will suggest that such a way of thinking and behaving is doomed. Consumers are already demonstrating that price is not the only factor behind them choosing one over another of the many similar offerings in the high streets and beyond. How they feel about a retailer or other company can also have an important effect.

Equally, the so-called Generation X employees, who are labelled self-centred for their refusal to knuckle down and go through all the hoops that their predecessors complained about, are perhaps just showing their dissatisfaction with the system. If the numbers of successful young entrepreneurs on both sides of the Atlantic are anything to go by, such people are perfectly capable of putting in the hours when they believe in what they are doing.

Straws in the wind such as the growing interest in 'stakeholders', the increasing discussion of 'purpose' and such emotions as 'passion' and 'trust', as well as the rising concern for the environment and ethics, suggest that change is already afoot. But, in Britain at least, cynicism and a conviction, in the face of the evidence, that the traditional ways are best live on.

This would not be so serious if Britain and the USA – to which it is much closer in business attitudes than its mainland European counterparts – were not so influential in the business world at large. US and UK companies and, more importantly, management consultancies are swarming into the countries of the former Soviet Union, Latin America and Asia, particularly China and India – bringing with them their 'tried and tested' ways of going about things.

The spread of deregulation and privatisation across western Europe means that differing national approaches to such aspects of business as service and funding are being swept away in the urge to make investments pay off in the ways approved of by Wall Street and the Square Mile. Many have responded with great gusto, throwing off the old cosy relationships between banks, large companies and the private companies that were seen as so vital to the strength of the German economy in particular, and embarking upon great acquisition sprees.

Just look at the levels of takeover and merger activity involving organisations from countries like Germany and France compared with only a few years ago. OK, they are not engaged in many hostile bids, but then neither are the British and the Americans: executives and their advisers have woken up to the fact that the only real beneficiaries of that sort of caper are the financial advisers and speculators who made the 1980s such an especially inglorious time, even by the standards of Anglo-Saxon business. In a series of agreed deals, companies that previously garnered little attention in the pages of *Fortune* or *Business Week* have swallowed up large chunks of the British investment banking industry and made significant inroads into the car industries of both Britain and the USA.

But there has also been fallout. As John Elkington, of the consultancy SustainAbility, relates in his book *Cannibals with Forks*, the giant German metals group Metallgesellschaft, was brought to earth after running up huge debts through speculating on the oil futures market, while police raids, investigations and prosecutions have cut across all sectors.

Even the mighty Deutsche Bank has seen its reputation tarnished by the combination of the activities of the property developer Jurgen Schneider, who amassed loans totalling billions of Deutschmarks, and those of Peter Young, the fund manager at the bank's London investment bank Morgan Grenfell, who seemingly tried too hard to keep up his impressive performance record.

Meanwhile, Japan, once – not so long ago – extolled as the place that really knows how to do it, seems to be plagued by one financial scandal after another and to suffer from just as artistic an approach to accounting as Britain did in the late 1980s. Companies are abandoning the idea of the job for life – and so spawning spates of suicides among middle-aged salarymen – cutting back on R&D investment and generally retrenching in the face of increasing competition from their operations in neighbouring countries.

Bob Garratt, author of the book *The Fish Rots from the Head* (a title claimed to be drawn from a Chinese proverb making the point that issues of ethics and governance are down to executives) says that 'all over the world the media is fixated by the lack of competence, unreliability, untrustworthiness and sheer greed of directors'.

And, as Elkington points out, 'leading business people may still be feted as heroes of the modern age, but growing numbers of people are wondering whether we can rely on capitalism to deliver anything like a sustainable future'. This is not a new concern, of course. Half a century ago, 'small is beautiful' champion Joseph Schumpeter noted the destructive element at the heart of capitalism. But what makes the human cost of the continuing reshaping of large tracts of international business so concerning at the moment is the awareness that it is not just about one company, sector or even region giving way to another. Everybody knows that, while technology is bringing great wealth to many, it is also likely to do many more out of work forever.

Even those who remain in work hardly behave as if they are thankful. A survey published in June 1998, at a time of great economic prosperity, suggested that the overwhelming majority of British workers were under increasing strain as a result of pressures at home and at work, with half regretting missing their children growing up or putting work before home or family. The study, covering male and female employees of various ages and levels of responsibility, claimed to be the largest ever undertaken into this area. But it was not alone in its findings.

Report after report has found great levels of stress and anxiety, even among those who are regarded by their bosses as most secure in their workplaces. Such surveys also indicate the real reason why women remain almost as rare in boardrooms as ever: modern business life is so demanding that it is nigh on impossible for two partners to work at any kind of level in an organisation and hold a family together. As the saying goes, something has to give – and it is usually the woman who gives up, so contributing to the lack of breadth that characterises many businesses.

Surveys like that conducted by WfD, a US consultancy specialising in helping organisations and employees balance work and life issues, also reveal personal sacrifices ranging from divorces and being absent from partners during serious illness to missing school fairs and not spending enough time on leisure or hobbies. A tenth of women interviewed in this particular research said they had postponed or forgone having children for the sake of the job and women were twice as likely as men to have difficulties forming relationships because of their work.

With what the researchers admit were surprising response levels among men, the survey puts renewed pressure on businesses and other organisations to move to break the 'long hours culture' and introduce new ways of working, or lose the people on whom they depend for future success.

According to Liz Bargh, UK chair of Ceridian Performance Partners, 'The report sends a clear signal – our present way of working is unsustainable, the cost is too high, in human terms and in business terms. Business will have to work with employees to balance work and life for compassion and competitiveness.'

As she did in her previous role as director of Opportunity 2000, the campaign to promote women in the workforce, Ms Bargh stresses that there is a 'business case', rather than just a moral reason for change.

Some are seeing a wider application of this principle. For example, Anthony Hilton, City editor of the London *Evening Standard*, wrote in his column of 12 November 1998 that an unacknowledged cause of the slowdown in consumer spending at that time was the widespread insecurity caused by changes to society and work patterns.

Pointing out that since the last boom people had had to adjust to the need to save seriously for their old age against a backcloth of a huge increase in workplace insecurity, he wrote: 'Is it any surprise that they should change their attitude to spending? They are simply playing back to the commercial sector the love of cost-cutting and economising that they have gleaned from it over the past few years.'

Put like that, it is not such a hard concept to understand that a business is more likely to thrive if its surroundings are prosperous. And yet at the moment, with few exceptions, such concepts as purpose, ethics and the environment are generally only asides in management thinking. It is as if those responsible feel that this sort of stuff might turn out to be fairly important at some later stage so they ought to include it, when in fact it is obvious – to this writer, anyway – that it is essential and central to the plot. It surely cannot be a coincidence that organisations that have remained innovative over long and successful lives tend to have better staff retention rates, to care about such things as treating people and their surroundings well and to have a clear sense of what they are doing and why.

In short, though management gurus might constantly suggest that they have discovered the *one* thing that differentiates one company from another, it is, in fact, the case that successful organisations tend to do *lots* of things right. They will be concerned about the environment, about ethics and about their people. But they will also be tremendously focused, highly driven and apt to keep a close eye on the finances.

In the following chapters readers will come across some notable examples of organisations seeking to live up to such ideals. These are the places where, in the words of an envious-sounding manager of a traditional company, 'there is a passion for the business'. When that passion exudes from not just the senior executives but from just about every employee – as seems to be the case in the organisations described – the stage is set for business to stop being a necessary evil and start becoming a genuine force for good that people working in it can feel positive about in much the same way as they traditionally do about working in hospitals and schools.

Anybody looking for evidence of how passionate business does not have to amount to unsuccessful business need go no further than *Fortune* magazine's annual survey of 'America's Most Admired Companies'.

As reporter Thomas A. Stewart relates, the USA's most admired companies – General Electric, Microsoft, Coca-Cola, Intel, Hewlett-Packard, Southwest Airlines, Berkshire Hathaway, Disney, Johnson & Johnson and Merck – do not just stand tall in terms of reputation, they also tower over the rest of corporate America in performance. Anybody who 10 years ago had put $1000 into each of the 10 companies would in 1998 have had a portfolio worth close on $150,000 – nearly three times more than if they had put $10,000 into Standard & Poor's 500.

And it does not stop there. The report points out that these companies are impressively good at employee relations, with Southwest Airlines topping *Fortune's* latest list of the 100 best companies to work for, and Microsoft, Merck and Hewlett-Packard all in the top 10.

Even when it comes to the currently voguish 'market value added' – a measure of how much wealth a company is creating for investors – GE, Microsoft, Coca-Cola, Intel and Merck take up the top five places, while in the area of sheer wealth created, GE, Coca-Cola and Microsoft form the top three of US corporations' market capitalisation. Got the picture?

Stewart stresses that the companies come from too many sectors for their success to be explained by the industries they are in – and suggests that the secret is leadership. Not any one style, but substance created from five main facets that together look a lot like what some might term passion, but 'passion' does not tell the whole story. While they are unmistakably totally committed to what they do, they also exude other related values, such as trust, confidence and respect, both in relation to themselves and to those with whom they deal, whether employees, customers, suppliers or the world at large.

What all this amounts to is a sense of engagement. And it is this that I believe separates the stars from the stragglers.

The companies identified by *Fortune*, and a growing band of others that are largely not yet so well-known, have found a way of operating that genuinely involves everybody pulling together (rather than in the traditional more condescending, patronising or paternalistic sense). In such organisations, there is little evidence of 'Us and Them' between executives and employees, between the company and the local community or between the company and its customers or suppliers. They have realised that the most effective route to success is by putting their efforts into what they do best – making things, selling things, providing services or whatever – and not diverting them into battles with various interest groups.

Some management commentators are starting to term this approach 'Co-opetition', after a book of that name by two US-based academics, so-called because it combines competition and co-operation in what, in the jargon, is said to be a 'win–win' situation. But, of course, like much that comes along in the management world, it is really just sound commonsense.

The problem with commonsense, of course, is that it is not nearly so easy to find as its name would suggest, and even those organisations that are confident enough to feel instinctively that they are doing the right thing sometimes need the encouragement of knowing that others are doing it and that it has received some sort of external verification through observers giving it a name.

Before exploring what such companies are doing and how it might alter negative perceptions of business, the book will set out how most of the business world, particularly that in the UK, looks to most people and how it got there. It will stop along the way to describe some of those most responsible for bringing the game of business into disrepute. And it will seek to explain how repeated management theories have not only failed to solve the problem – despite containing nuggets of truth – but have generally made it worse, simply through deepening the cynicism when they do not deliver what is promised.

The approach of the millennium has seen management consultants and business school academics return time and again to two main and related themes: business is changing faster than ever before; and the only constant is change. For all this turmoil, however, they themselves do not seem to have changed that much in recent years.

Sure, they make whizzier presentations, utilising all the latest developments in technology, and like the rest of us they work in a slightly more frenzied way than before. But they do not appear to have moved on from the conviction that life and, in particular, business can be explained by reference to complicated analyses that are given three-letter acronyms.

The flow of supposedly new concepts casting light on aspects of organisational behaviour, customer habits or business trends shows no sign of abating. Yet, at the same time, it becomes more and more obvious – albeit, to still too few people – that, while on the surface at least we have become highly sophisticated, the fundamentals of business have changed little since true visionaries such as William McKnight of 3M and Bill Hewlett and David Packard of Hewlett-Packard set down the principles by which they would run their organisations.

Basically, these amounted to the conviction that, if you treat people right, they will do a good job. Such ideas were revolutionary enough at the time they were introduced – back in the early years of this century – but they still stand in pretty marked contrast to the attitudes of the vast majority of businesses. While they talk fine language about 'empowerment' and 'learning organisations', most executives still subscribe to much of the command-and-control thinking that implies that it is best if employees leave their brains – and especially their values – at the door. Consequently, at the very time that they are regretting the lack of initiative or entrepreneurial flair within their organisations, they are busily reinforcing the mechanisms that prevent such attitudes from even gaining a hold, let alone flourishing.

This somewhat downcast view of business and work in general was epitomised when a writer in the *Financial Times* criticised a book for suggesting that work could be fun or cool. Such a view, it implied, misunderstood the nature of work in that this was an activity that was supposed to be dull and uninspiring; otherwise it would not be work.

Now, the clear focus of that book, and others of its type, was on the 'new' industries springing up in places such as Silicon Valley. And it was implicit that the thinking exemplified by the FT writer was old fashioned. Yet this is also a misunderstanding.

Attitudes to work are not about time or, for that matter, place. They are dependent on the ways in which it is done and on whether those doing it feel it is worthwhile. Put that way, Thomas Edison and those alongside him probably had a lot more fun, excitement and pure thrills than many of those people working in state-of-the-art software publishers do today.

Similarly, this book will seek to show that working in a steel plant run by a company like Nucor can be a lot more exciting than slaving away in a 'cool' industry such as bicycle manufacture, if the company you are working for is striving to compete at the bottom end of the market.

It is all a question of attitude and culture. Of engagement. Or, rather, of a lack of it.

It is this book's contention that we in Britain have been the victims of a gigantic scam. It has very little to do with privatisation and a lot to do with what is increasingly clearly a misrepresentation of the country's industrial wellbeing. Flushed with the soaring profits achieved on the back of what has often been termed the 'benign economic climate' of the mid-1990s,

Britain's bosses were busy patting themselves on the back and awarding themselves impressive 'internationally competitive' pay rises even as the squeals of protest over the strength of the pound from what still remained of the manufacturing sector began to indicate that perhaps all was not as well as was thought. (Incidentally, is it not odd how companies seem much quicker to blame falling profits on the strength of the pound than they are to attribute rising earnings to its weakness.)

By the time McKinsey's damning productivity report was out, the game was well and truly up. As Simon Philips of Bridgewater, a management consultancy specialising in helping companies to manage growth, points out, many companies had failed to make the most of the advantageous conditions and were very poorly placed to withstand another downturn, simply because the most obvious remedy – cutting costs – had already been used up.

Britain's bosses are failing us because, having spent years assuring everybody that massive redundancy programmes were over because they were part of a necessary restructuring that was now complete, they are showing a troubling readiness to embark on just such exercises all over again in the hope of shoring up their tottering kingdoms for just a little longer.

By failing to exploit the opportunities of recent years and so soar to greater things, they have left those companies not already in overseas hands vulnerable to takeover from much more solid-looking enterprises from the USA, a rejuvenated Germany and even France. Even now that the McKinsey report has brought on a bout of collective soul-searching, the emphasis seems to be on the wrong things.

The problem with focusing on productivity, as Hugo Dixon pointed out in the *Financial Times* of 21 August 1998, is that it can lead to a concentration on cutting costs in the name of efficiency and profitability rather than increasing the amount produced. 'Mr Brown's focus on productivity sends the wrong message,' he writes. 'It gives the impression that all he wants is for industry to grind down further on its cost base. It would be better if he told them to move on to the front foot: invest more in equipment, training and marketing. Be ambitious.'

This, above all, requires action rather than rhetoric. And one of the key reasons why Britain's executives failed to make the most of what looked like halcyon days just a little while later is that, on the whole, they failed to understand that words counted for nothing if they could not engage their employees, their suppliers, their customers and the societies in which they operated.

An ability to engage in this way is a large part of that hard-to-define something that explains why one company fails and another succeeds, or why one stops succeeding and another appears from nowhere. And Britain's companies clearly need to pay a lot more attention to it as we embark on the 21st century.

This book will argue that only by following what might be termed 'the rules of engagement' can British business really hope to compete with the best in the world. Engagement comes in many guises, but I suggest that at the heart of the concept there are just six basic tenets – passion, commitment, sense of purpose, core values, integrity and respect.

The following pages will describe how so many British corporations, professional services firms and public-sector organisations are lacking some or all of these principles – with devastating results, not just for those unfortunate enough to work for such organisations but for us all.

With many executives seemingly intent on a sort of zero-sum game that involves them driving their employees ever harder for ever-diminishing rewards and security – while unable to understand why the market for their goods and services is declining – it would be easy to be pessimistic and conclude that it will all end badly. Happily, however, enough organisations in Britain and overseas are realising that business success is about a lot more than short-term profits.

These are not – as was briefly the craze a few years back – small organisations headed by crusading founders suggesting that saving some obscure species of rainforest fern is more important than producing a return for shareholders. For the most part, these are regular enterprises recognisable as businesses to us all that are showing how tempering the profit motive with a sense of their place in the community makes much better business sense than pretending you are operating in a vacuum.

Chapter 1

TALK ABOUT
THE PASSION

Passion might seem an odd thing to accuse business leaders of lacking. Passion, some might say, is what you feel for your spouse and family, for football, for music – but not for work.

And that is precisely the problem. In far too many of Britain's businesses employees of all levels seem to have left all notions of caring and devotion at home. At work, they seem to think, just doing enough to get by will do.

The words 'passion' and 'passionate' are bandied about, usually by proprietors of companies selling premium sandwiches – the highly successful Pret à Manger – or exotic coffee – Starbucks, US owner of the Seattle Coffee Company. And good luck to them. If being passionate about what is otherwise a commodity product can enable you effectively to create a new market, with its share of imitators, and charge premium prices, it is somewhat odd and hugely disappointing that others do not cotton on to the power of such basic emotions.

Nowhere is this more obvious than in customer service. Years of programmes and initiatives established at the urging of a limitless list of gurus have created a process for doing the work that is undoubtedly more effective – in most cases – than the old way. Utilities, under the pressure of private ownership, have, of course, improved immeasurably – even to the extent of realising that not all of their customers are able to sit in their homes all day on the off-chance that they might meet an appointment.

But these improvements do not go very far. They are only skin deep. Instead of having a real zeal about getting the job done, the staff in what are laughingly called customer service centres are really concerned about meeting their targets for calls answered, sales made and the rest. And who can blame them? If that is how they are being rewarded that is how they are going to behave.

All those British bosses who have travelled to the United States and seen the customer service revolution in action have noted the plastic smiles and the 'have a nice day nows', but have missed the fact that what really works in this environment is a proper realisation of the importance of responding to – or, better yet, anticipating – a customer's needs and demands rather than merely trying to get him or her to buy what you have to sell.

It is no accident that the Carphone Warehouse has succeeded so spectacularly in the mobile telephone business. It has risen above an industry that is as cut-throat as selling second-hand cars through demanding that its sales people treat customers as individual people rather than mugs to be sold the latest package. And employees will only respond to such urgings if they are remunerated accordingly – i.e. not on the number of sales recorded each hour.

Sadly, the Carphone Warehouse is not typical of the British high street. So aghast is founder Charles Dunstone at attitudes in much of his sector that he will not hire from rival companies. But, given the approach to selling in many other retail outlets, it would not be surprising if Dunstone extended his ban far more widely.

British retailers *have* learned from their American cousins that it is OK to have sales more frequently than a few days after Christmas. But they seem to have picked up very little else.

Instead, they spend a lot of time – particularly in the run-up to the Christmas period that is so vital to their profitability – complaining about the slowness of sales, seemingly oblivious to the fact that they turn away lots of opportunities to do business simply because they have become so enamoured of the notion of Just-in-Time supplies that they have insufficient stock with which to satisfy all but the most mainstream of demands.

> *Retailers are stuck in some kind of time warp where consumers have so much time that they do not mind returning to the shop several times in the coming weeks in the hope that the item they require might have miraculously reappeared.*

They seem to allow this to happen because they are stuck in some kind of time warp, where consumers have so much time that they do not mind returning to the shop several times in the coming weeks in the hope that the item they require might have miraculously reappeared. (In fact, it is more likely to have been discontinued.) Have they not heard about this being the age of instant gratification?

Even if they had, they would not worry. Quite the contrary. So confident are they that the general public owes them a living that – rather like those people who put signs in their windows 'regretting' that they cannot open at times when they might gain custom or do things that might be construed as a service – they are often quite smug in their inability to sell something. It is the 'nothing to do with me, guv' syndrome.

Companies such as Marks & Spencer and the John Lewis Partnership have well-deserved reputations for providing value and for investing a great deal in their workforces. But when it comes to a true dedication to serving the customer, rather than going through the motions of customer service processes, they struggle in comparison with the likes of the Gap.

A *Financial Times* examination of the experience of shopping in London's doom-laden Oxford Street in the run-up to Christmas 1998 found the US-based store to offer a rare ray of light. Staff were determined to help, found the reporter. It was an experience shared by a relative of mine who – not finding the right size in the item she saw in her local store – had an assistant volunteer to find it at another store – and then, on hearing it was needed for an imminent event, offer to arrange for it to be collected and sent by cab to her home. That is passion at work.

Likewise, American Express has realised that if that little rectangle of plastic is really of value to you then you can ill-afford to be without it. Accordingly, when mine was stolen, I had a replacement sent to me by bike within 24 hours. Needless to say, replacements for the other cards took somewhat longer to arrive.

Making such things happen apparently so effortlessly takes a great deal of work. It is a lot more complicated than those slogans about hiring 'nice people rather than training people to be nice' imply. But it can be done.

It requires giving staff a clear indication of what the object of the exercise is and letting them know that – within certain parameters – they make the decisions about achieving it.

EVEN STEEL WORKERS CAN BE PASSIONATE

Such attitudes are common enough in the start-ups of California's Silicon Valley and the UK's Cambridge area, but they are a little unusual in a traditional industry such as steel, where management tends to see employees as something to be hired at a minimum cost to do the jobs that machines will not yet do – and certainly unworthy of being involved in decision-making. At Nucor, though, Ken Iverson and his colleagues have managed to put flesh on the bones of the hackneyed mantra 'our people are our greatest asset' and make it work.

Unlike Virgin, HP and 3M – which all have long histories of this sort of approach – Nucor is the more remarkable for having come around to this way of thinking relatively recently. As with those other organisations, though, the impetus was visionary leadership.

The original omens were not good. As he recounts in his book, Iverson believes his main qualification for being appointed head of what was then called Nuclear Corporation of America at the age of 37 was the fact that he was running the company's one profitable division – a steel joist maker in Florence, South Carolina called Vulcraft. He was filling the shoes of a man who had resigned at a time when the company had defaulted on two major loan payments and, with losses running at $400,000 a year on sales of $20m, was facing bankruptcy.

A graduate of the prestigious Cornell University with a masters degree in mechanical engineering, Iverson had previously worked in the Mid-West, first in the research centre for construction and agricultural machinery maker International Harvester, then at an Indiana steel products company and finally at Michigan's Cannon Muskegon Corporation, where he developed a high-temperature sheeting material used on the Mercury manned space capsule to protect it when it re-entered the Earth's atmosphere. But he does not match the stereotype of an industrial engineer. As an immensely practical man, with a fondness for pointing out the lessons learned from such episodes as fixing his father's car after crashing it into a tree, he appears to have an innate sense of how to get the best out of people.

When he took on his new role – a job that, he insists, became his by default because nobody else wanted it – he quickly found that not much was expected of him. 'Nuclear's shareholders had all but given up hope. They assumed the company was a goner, no matter what I did, so the prevailing attitude was, "If it doesn't cost anything, sure try it".'

As a result, he and Sam Spiegel, the chief financial officer who played an important supporting role in the transformation of a company that had been dabbling in various sectors in an attempt to survive, quickly sold off the parts of the company that were unprofitable and shifted their attention to the Vulcraft operations in Florence and in Norfolk, Nebraska, where a second joist plant had recently been built.

'Our strategy was what executives now call "focusing on our core competencies", although that's not what we called it', recalls Iverson with characteristic bluntness. 'We just placed the few chips we had left on the businesses that were turning a buck.'

The shift of emphasis produced a swift improvement in the figures, but the dramatic changes since the summer of 1965 had left the employees in a state of shock. According to the company's official history, *The Legend of Nucor Corporation*, Iverson's response on 1 November of that year was to send every employee a letter in which the company's direction was outlined.

He wrote that rapid growth in sales, 'coupled with other problems', had created a need for the realignment of the company seen in the establishment of four divisions. But he also pointed out that the company needed to adopt a new way of doing business.

Just as he had demonstrated a belief in communicating with employees long before it became fashionable, so he set in motion the creation of a flat organisation decades before 'delayering' and 'empowerment' became management watchwords.

In a magazine interview years later, Iverson explained the four principles on which this reorganisation was based and to which he attributed the company's success. The first was having few management layers – there are just four, from the chief executive, via vice-presidents and general managers on the third rung and department managers on the second, to supervisors. The second was a minimum of staff people – at headquarters there are just 22, while at the Berkeley plant in South Carolina, for example, there is a team of about six managers who spread responsibility for such tasks as finance and human resources between them.

According to Rex Query, one of the six managers at this newest of the company's steel plants, this has the advantage of forcing managers like himself to be hands off, simply because they do not have the time to get involved in the nitty-gritty of each area. Moreover, because he and his colleagues know that the company is not going to hire a lot of people there is no danger of the sort of bureaucracy that is generally regarded as so debilitating for large businesses growing up. 'We keep it very simple rather than creating an empire. We don't make things complex that don't have to be.'

The third success factor was pushing responsibilities down to the lowest possible level and the final one was the use of strong incentives to focus everyone – and not just executives – on productivity and earnings.

The former – devolving responsibility – is closely allied with the previous two. Many organisations talk about doing this, but at Nucor it can be seen at the plants. In the spring of 1998 the Berkeley operation was still in its infancy and as such somewhat liable to breakdowns and other problems, but a visitor wandering around would still have been struck by the fact that the employees were just getting on with tasks rather than being shouted at by foremen. Employees clearly knew what they had to do and the fact that they acted on this knowledge with more than the usual enthusiasm seen in manufacturing operations was probably not unrelated to Iverson's last success factor – incentives linked to productivity and earnings.

This is born of Iverson's conviction that it is no good executives having bonuses, stock options and other increasingly complex incentive schemes if those in the front line feel that they earn the same no matter how much they get paid. As he states in *Plain Talk*, compensation has been the key to fostering teamwork, a concept with which, as he adds, many companies have in recent years been grappling – with varying degrees of success.

'The root of their frustration, I suspect, may be that their compensation systems still reward individual contributions more than they reward teamwork. Some also tie variable compensation to silly goals that have little to do with the real work people must perform for the business to be productive and profitable,' he writes.

> *Instead of sending their people off to seminars to close their eyes and fall into one another's arms, maybe these companies should restructure compensation to ensure that people who work together, earn together.*

'Instead of sending their people off to seminars to close their eyes and fall into one another's arms, maybe these companies should restructure compensation to ensure that people who work together, earn together.'

The way it works at Nucor is that production workers are typically paid two-thirds to three-quarters of the industrial average as a basic wage, but they have the opportunity to earn much more in bonuses that are paid weekly. Not for nothing, do Iverson and his fellow managers describe such bonuses as 'at risk' pay: as he puts it in his book, because of the low base pay levels, production workers start each day with no guarantee that they will earn a competitive wage. But so effective is the simple formula that there appears to be little actual risk; in the last couple of years, workers at steel mills in South Carolina, for example, have been earning up to twice as much again as their base pay – taking their annual earnings to an average of $60,000 and making them the best paid employees in their industry.

Iverson does not claim credit for inventing the system. A version was at Vulcraft before he became a manager there in the early 1960s and because it seemed to work well, he took it, refined it a little and spread it to the whole company when he took over several years later.

Now, he says that employees must do just two things to earn such bonuses: work in teams and produce. In fact, it is a little more complicated than that – but not much. Teams of workers, say a 20-strong melting and casting crew in a steel mill, will have established for them a 'production baseline' – meaning what they will be expected to achieve as a team in a shift. This baseline is based on what the machinery at their disposal is deemed capable of and what experience says they should be able to do. Care is taken to set production figures that are realistic; that is, tough to achieve, but within a team's reach. 'We want the teams to get a taste of the bonus because, once they do, they always stretch for more', adds Iverson.

Many people would wonder how paying employees so well on a consistent basis enables the company to continue to outdo its competitors. But Nucor has a simple explanation. Iverson quotes one of the company's general managers as saying that, while most businesses focus on what a person makes, 'we think what matters is how much labour cost goes into the product. If we pay our people twice what a competitor pays, but that opportunity to earn more motivates them to produce three times as many joists per hour, our joists cost less.'

Indeed, in 1996, the company's employment costs, including fringe benefits, were less than $40 per ton of steel produced, or roughly half the total for the big steel companies. 'Our people earn more because they're more efficient and more productive. We didn't make them that way. We just structured compensation to give them a clear incentive and turned them loose. We've trusted in their ingenuity to keep us competitive. And they haven't let us down,' writes Iverson.

The power of this approach is clear to any observer. A steel mill like the one in Berkeley County, near the classic southern city of Charleston, is no place for a touchy-feely management style. It is hot and noisy with plenty of potential for appalling accidents. And yet there is an obvious sense of a workforce at one with itself and full of passion about what it is doing.

Though the bonus system may imply that employees spend their eight-hour shifts working flat out in the quest for targets, the reality is more one of quiet deliberation rather than frantic rushing about. In a workplace that is a curious mixture of the latest high-tech equipment and tough manual labour, teams of workers go about their tasks with an easy confidence. There is so little direction from above that it is easy to see why Query says that managers like himself are 'just support for the guys that produce', adding: 'I'm overhead and Iverson is overhead – if you forget that you get your priorities all wrong.'

In keeping with this attitude, Iverson says that the company supplies equipment, training, benefits and 'other fundamental support' and leaves the rest up to the group. 'So, in a sense, each group is in business for itself. Work groups set their own goals for exceeding the baseline and work out their own ways of pursuing them, guided only by this certainty: the more they produce, the more they earn. They have a simple stake in the business.'

Claiming that, 'like most successful entrepreneurs', the company's employees are enthusiastic, energetic and dead earnest about their work, Iverson points to the example of a Vulcraft worker who says his shift team habitually arrives for work about 45 minutes before the shift is due to start. 'It's like a football team before a game,' says the worker. 'You don't show up for the kick-off. You get there early and you get yourself ready. When that horn blows, we have to be primed. We've got eight hours to make us some money. The more we get done, the more we make.'

Though some might see this as indicative of a money-fixated regime, the clear focus created by these incentives is also behind the name the workers give to the hooter that sounds when the great rolling machinery grinds into action at the Berkeley plant. 'We call it "the money horn", because it means we're going to make money,' says Brian Kurtz, the facility's accountant. In other words, everybody – whether at the front line or in a supporting role – fully accepts the notion that they only make money when the machinery is in action; everything else is purely supplementary.

This is not to say that such an approach to employees has been entirely trouble-free. Over the years, Nucor has been much criticised by trade unionists and defenders of Big Steel on the grounds that it has created an unlevel playing field by deliberately siting its plants in rural, traditionally non-union areas and so not being bound by the various restrictions – particularly, demarcation lines – imposed by unions.

Nucor's line – as set out in the official company history – has been that unions exist less to protect the interests of ordinary workers than to create good life styles for their officers. Employees at one of the company's divisions in Alabama were reminded of this when they were recruited by the Ironworkers International Union and Shopmen's Local 539 in 1968 – so setting off a bruising battle between management and the union that ended in victory for the company late the following year.

Iverson believes that the company remains union-free to this day because – as he told the *Wall Street Journal* in 1981 – even the most lucrative basic steel agreement with a union cannot match the combination of wages and job security offered by Nucor.

In fact, adds *The Legend of Nucor*, he does not object to the union pay scales so much as the work rules which he feels that – in setting strict parameters on each job category – hobble workers and stifle productivity.

Moreover, while he insists that the potential to earn significant salaries is the best motivator, especially for people who have often not previously enjoyed high pay, Iverson also puts a lot of store by the absence of a 'them and us' culture at Nucor.

One of his first actions on taking over at Vulcraft back in the early 1960s had been to do away with the old Southern practice of separate washrooms for black and white workers. When given control of the whole company, he went further – not just stripping out layers of management but also abolishing such traditional management perks as executive dining rooms and parking spaces, and giving everybody the same insurance and holiday benefits. So complete is the lack of hierarchy that the visitor to a Nucor plant such as Berkeley can find it hard to find the management suite; it is not defined by a smart reception area or a line of company cars outside.

This policy of equality also works when times get tough. In the early 1980s, when – as Iverson relates in *Plain Talk* – a dark era saw the number of steel workers in America halve, from 400,000 to 200,000, individuals' earnings were cut by about a quarter as the company reduced the working week in line with the fall in demand for its products. But the company says it got through the crisis without laying off a single worker, not through altruism but through a policy that Iverson calls 'painsharing'.

'We not only shared the pain, we doled out the lion's share to the people at the top,' he writes. He points out that department heads took cuts of up to 40 per cent and that general managers and other company officers earned about half of the sums they received in previous years. Iverson's own pay plunged from about $450,000 to $110,000.

The reason for adopting this solution to the problem is purely businesslike. 'To compete over the long term, a company needs loyal, motivated employees,' he writes, adding that managers – including some in his own industry – who have seen their earnings rise as those of the companies they run fall cannot expect this to happen if they go on dropping people as soon as the going gets a little hard.

> 'To compete over the long term, a company needs loyal, motivated employees.'

Iverson feels so strongly about this issue that in a 1985 interview he described how in 1970 he went against his usual policy of not interfering with the management of the company's various divisions after a general manager responded to slow business by laying off 40 employees. He ordered the manager never to lay off a worker again and, according to the company's official history, saw that most of the employees were back working for the company within a year.

If this does not sound like the sort of behaviour to be expected of a 'union-bashing' company, Iverson and his colleagues are adamant that nobody should run away with the idea that Nucor is some kind of soft touch. Steel is – and will remain – an intensely competitive business, and, like those operating companies at the more high-tech end of industry, Nucor's executives know that the only way they can stay ahead of the chasing pack is to remain highly profitable and innovative – both of which require good people working in an open atmosphere.

Company managers explain their antipathy to unions on the basis that they get in the way of the incentive programmes that fire the company's various operations. Rex Query says that the company values attitude above everything else – taking the view that skills can be taught.

And though the sort of low-key approach that has seen Iverson answer the headquarters phones after the receptionist has gone home in the evening has come to be regarded as 'Nucor culture', it is not as resistant to outsiders as some. Both Rodney Mott, general manager of Berkeley, and John Correnti, who in 1995 took over from Iverson as chief executive, began their careers with US Steel.

SIZE DOES NOT MATTER

British Steel has frequently been hailed as an example of how a former state-owned operator can turn itself from a bloated organisation into a highly efficient one. But, profitable as it has become, it is still very much at the mercy of the 'cycle' that supposedly governs the steel industry.

The company says it has learned a great deal from Nucor and other mini-mills in the USA. But it nonetheless gives the impression that, professional as its managers are, they are someway short of being masters of their own destiny.

Yet it does not have to be that way. The about-turn at Nucor is not an isolated example – even in its own industry. A Texas-based mini-mill called Chaparral Steel has also been celebrated by management writers for much the same reasons as Nucor. More significant, perhaps, is the way in which AK Steel has been inspired to transform itself. When US steel industry veteran Thomas Graham took over the company in 1992, it was, he says, 'the worst steel company in the world'. Losing $40 to $50 a ton at a time when the rest of the struggling industry was losing about half that, it faced insolvency through being unable to meet bank loans that were coming due. By the late 1990s, the company had not only moved away from the brink of collapse but was expanding – at the premium end of the market.

Pointing out that Graham has achieved this despite AK being a century-old company with a unionised workforce in the heart of the rust belt rather than 'a start-up with a shiny new mill and a compliant, non-union workforce in a southern state', journalist John Holusha says in a 1997 issue of Booz-Allen & Hamilton's *Strategy & Business* magazine that the story 'offers lessons for managers no matter how far their companies are from the rust belt'.

As Holusha describes it, 'AK's comeback is a classic case of crisis control, one that involved the deployment of a new team of savvy executives to rebuild strategy and see to its execution.'

The team was aided by a certain amount of good luck in that, as it was embarking on the rescue effort, big steel consumers increased their demand. The German luxury car makers BMW and Mercedes-Benz set up manufacturing facilities in the USA, while Japanese companies expanded operations. Such moves have helped increase the proportion of US-made cars and light trucks, from 10.7 million out of 15 million total sales in the late 1980s, to about 12 million out of the same number. Moreover, automobile industry suppliers reckon that the number of cars and light trucks made in the USA will increase by more than one million a year over the next few years – and, with the overseas companies pledging to use local steel rather than ship in components from their home bases, that can only be good news for the US steel industry.

Even so, the executives– in much the same way as Iverson and his associates – had to challenge past assumptions. This was the cause of the plant shutdowns and the adjustment of the company's product mix. It also accounted for a determination to wrest control from Kawasaki Steel of Japan, which in 1989 had taken a half share of the troubled business then known as Armco Steel from the parent company Armco.

But when Graham and his colleagues began work in 1992 their aims were much more basic. As Holusha puts it, much of what Graham did initially was 'textbook turnaround tactics'. He replaced the existing managers with those that he had grown to trust during his legendary career in the steel industry, including current chief executive Richard Wardrop. He sold off non-essential assets – including the company golf course – and he got outside contractors to take on such peripheral activities as security.

Moreover, in keeping with the determination to challenge assumptions, he brought an outsider's eye to the running of the company. Accordingly, he rejected the long-held idea that both of AK's plants – at Middletown, Ohio and Ashland, Kentucky – had to be treated equally and he acted swiftly to improve the company's competitiveness by abandoning, within a month of taking over, a costly practice that had been used to prop up a problematic production process.

As a veteran of some of the country's biggest mills, Graham could see that the company was burdened by its costs. Through operating too much equipment for the amount of steel that it was shipping, AK was needing 6.5 man-hours to make a ton of steel, compared with about half that at the average integrated mill and less than 1 man-hour at mini-mills like those operated by Nucor.

Significantly, Wardrop – who was charged with improving productivity – did not blame the workforce for the uncompetitive performance. According to Holusha's account, he said the problem lay with managers who did not believe productivity could be improved.

> *The workforce was not blamed for the uncompetitive performance. It was acknowledged that the problem lay with managers who did not believe productivity could be improved.*

After they were replaced with people with greater vision, Middletown soon found itself rolling 300,000 tons a month, compared with 200,000 tons before. More recently, the figure has been more like 420,000 to 430,000 tons.

But, of course, improvements in productivity would count for little if there were not a market for the steel. And here Graham has shown himself an enemy of the lowest-common-denominator school of business.

He made his name when he revived the US Steel operations at USX Corporation in the late 1980s, at a time when they were losing $1 billion a year. His technique was to close obsolete plants and concentrate on products for which a company making steel from raw ore, rather than the scrap used by the mini-mills, had a competitive advantage. This meant letting Nucor and other mini-mills have the market for low-value products, such as the bars used to reinforce concrete in roads, and concentrating on higher-quality sheet steel. By taking this approach and focusing on a market where the integrated mills using blast furnaces have an advantage through their ability to control the quality of the product, he is credited with giving the big companies a life line.

And he took the same sort of tack at AK – in the words of one observer, making 'more efficient and productive use of its existing integrated technology to produce high-quality, value-added products that command healthy prices'.

Contrast this determination to shape their own futures with the much more common reliance on outside factors. Given such an inability to control events around them, it is a little surprising that the leaders of big steel throughout the world command such high salaries.

Come to that, too often in too many industries too many executives seem to be just marking time – as if they know that nothing they do will make a difference. No wonder Scott Adams, creator of the 'Dilbert' cartoon feels that managers are largely harmless, locked into a routine of meetings, training courses and paper-pushing that has little importance to the scheme of things.

However, even a lumbering giant like Britain's GEC can change its approach. Lord Weinstock, the man who built it up, has retired. And, although the new management was felt to have started by continuing in the same vein, closing down factories, shutting research and development facilities and laying off staff, it has apparently responded to the changes in the air.

Indeed, in the middle of 1997 – several months after he had taken over running GEC from Weinstock – George (later Lord) Simpson laid out the results of a strategic review of the company that, in the words of Weinstock biographer Stephen Aris, indicated that the new man 'intended to demolish most of the foundations on which Weinstock's creation had rested'. The signs were that the famous cash mountain would be reduced, the amount spent on product development increased and the company overall given better focus.

Though 1998 saw certain parts of the plan brought into action, it also saw a certain amount of confusion, as the company – in yet another example of an organisation losing control of its own fate – suddenly sought to become involved in the mergers that were aimed at reshaping the European defence industry.

The real problem, though, is that GEC under its new leadership has yet to excite in the same way as its US near-namesake. This is possibly just a matter of time, but it could also be something to do with the fact that Simpson does not appear to have that personal spark that engages people. Moreover, nor does he have a product that fires the imagination in the way that some of those from the likes of similarly sprawling companies do, such as 3M and HP – even though, besides its well-known defence businesses, GEC is involved in the high-growth telecommunications industry.

> *At companies such as British Steel each set of figures tends to be accompanied by announcements of fresh job cuts, as it embarks on the same route towards maintaining profitability as BT did in the 1980s.*

BACK-PEDALLING

But it is not just big old industry that has found itself exposed to new challenges and threats. Being in an exciting field is also not enough on its own to ensure success. Though established for more than a century, the bicycle industry has always been small scale, with many comparatively well-known marques little more than garage operations. Yet, rather than make them flexible and responsive in the way that management writers tend to assume that small operations are, this state has largely made them vulnerable to larger and more efficient operations that can charge lower prices.

The extent to which this informal approach to business had survived into the late 20th century was made apparent when the new managing director of a reputable manufacturer found it impossible to come up with reliable statistics on the state of the market. The business was so fragmented and limited in scope that it was subjected to only the most cursory of surveys.

No doubt because of this lack of professionalism, the British cycle industry – though responsible for some of the great names of the past, such as Raleigh, Dawes, Claud Butler and the like – has lately been consigned to being little more than a bit player in a game increasingly dominated by companies from the Far East and the USA. In 1998, Tandem, hit by losses of more than £2m, set about selling its well-known Townsend, Falcon and British Eagle brands and moved into running racecourses, while even Italian and French marques make little impression beyond the confines of the very specialist field of road racing.

The casual observer may well not recognise this bleak picture. He or she might point to the fact that some of the old-familiar names are often on display inside the apparently increasing numbers of bicycle shops, and wonder how it can be argued that the industry is hurting.

And it is true that Raleigh – which, incidentally, was still US-owned at the end of 1998 following a spell within the conglomerate TI – has picked itself up in recent years and even produces a few bikes that impress the experts. But it is in no way at the cutting edge. Indeed, at one point cycling insiders used to snigger at the company's glossy newspaper advertisements pushing the mountain biking lifestyle out of the conviction that Raleigh had such a bad name in the sport that all the commercials did was aid their competitors by boosting interest in it in general.

The problem for Raleigh is that without the kudos that comes from being seen as a trend setter in the increasingly dominant segment of mountain biking, it has been forced to compete with a huge variety of domestic and imported marques on price – something for which its long-held reputation for quality ill-equips it.

Conscious perhaps that industry commentators are constantly pointing out that innovation and specialisation are the only ways out of such an impasse, Raleigh has lately come up with a bike that uses an electric engine to give riders a little boost when the going gets tough, while other manufacturers are seeking to exploit the interest in family cycling by producing modern-day tourers.

Hitherto, such efforts appear to have enjoyed only limited success. Raleigh has been able to build on its reputation for reliability to gain a toehold in the still highly important off-road sector of the market, but without that certain 'coolness' possessed by the industry upstarts, it is destined to compete with the more mass-market producers – largely on the basis of price.

The result has been that, even where it is trying to be a little innovative – it is vulnerable to a lower-cost entrant. For example, the semi-motorised bike would appear to have a market among the middle-aged and beyond, but well-known inventor and bike fan Sir Clive Sinclair has come up with a removable engine pack that promises the same sort of benefits as the Raleigh at a lower price.

Equally, other strugglers in the highly fragmented bicycle business have been learning that logic does not always play a large part in business – or anywhere else. Pushing the notion of the family touring bike may appear sound, but it is in fact flying in the face of reality – as anybody who has witnessed the guffaws when a cycle shop employee is told that that road bikes are making a comeback will know. The sort of bikes envisaged might be much more suitable for road riding than the fat-tired cycles that have lately been put to that use, but if they do not create the same sort of excitement as the increasingly high-tech American dream machines that is an irrelevance.

To be fair, this is not just yet another example of a British tendency to rest on one's laurels and allow venerable names of the past to become just that rather than vibrant brands with rich histories. The US company Schwinn was even more guilty of failing to read the signs – and it was much closer to the action, since the craze first for BMX dirt bikes and then mountain bikes began in its backyard – albeit several hundreds of miles from the company's then Chicago headquarters.

Moreover, as journalists Judith Crown and Glenn Coleman explain in *No Hands*, their entertaining account of 'the rise and fall of an American institution', the company was not unaware of what was going on in California back in the early 1970s. Dealers in the state sent back urgent reports of a growing number of mavericks customising old cycles (often Schwinns) for use on the trails around Mount Tamalpais and other peaks in the San Francisco area, and the company even despatched engineers to see for themselves what was going on. But the company decided it was all going to be a localised and short-lived fad and kept itself aloof from developments that have transformed the cycle industry, not just in the USA but around the world.

By making cycling 'cool', Gary Fisher, Tom Ritchey and other pioneering off-roaders were instrumental in bringing cycling out of back-alley shops and into modern retail centres. Thanks to the coincidence with increasing interest in both the environment and physical fitness, affluent people who hitherto had seen bicycles as something they left behind once they could drive started buying something that was fun – and good for them. Moreover, they showed an amazing willingness to part with serious sums of money to partake of it.

While many people would see a cycle as a low-cost form of transport, this new breed of consumers was ready to spend hundreds of dollars or pounds on not just the basic equipment but also the accessories, which – as with many other industries – is where the manufacturers really make their money. This had the knock-on effect of luring in designers, engineers and marketers who otherwise would not have looked twice at the industry. To this day, catalogues produced by the leading edge names – now often part of larger organisations – stress the innovation and technology that goes into the equipment on display.

One of the most obvious ways in which this trend has manifested itself is in the development of full-suspension bikes. Shock absorbers had been available for the front forks for some time before various companies started tinkering with designs for cushioning the rear too.

The resulting machines – many of which had a 'Y' shape – were initially targeted at the serious mountain biking crowd, but have increasingly been taken up by urban types, partly, of course, because they are regarded as being cool, but also because they can claim – with rather more justification than their fellow townies tooling around in off-road vehicles – that they help deal with the cities' increasingly pot-holed roads.

To illustrate the extent to which cycling has lured in talent that would traditionally have been expected to keep its distance, the most popular affordable full-suspension bike of the late 1990s was designed by a British engineer who had previously worked for the Benetton motor racing team. For Jon Whyte, a large part of the attraction of shifting allegiance to cycling was in being able to work on a whole project rather than being – to coin a phrase – a mere cog in the wheel of a large Formula One set-up. It also helped that he himself – though a keen cyclist – was getting to an age where he put greater emphasis on the comfort provided by suspension on both wheels. It is perhaps typical, though, that he is signed to the US company Marin, albeit through its UK distributor, rather than Raleigh or one of its UK rivals.

Tom Ritchey, one of the pioneers of what was to become mountain biking, presaged what in recent years has often been said of Britain's Raleigh with the quip: 'When cycling became serious, people did not think Schwinn.'

While Schwinn was imploding – largely as a result of its own complacency – two companies, in particular, were growing up in its place. Giant, the Taiwan company that in the 1970s hardly lived up to its name in terms of size, became increasingly ubiquitous – making bikes not just for others but increasingly under its own name. More embarrassingly for Schwinn, Trek – based not far from the old-established company's original Chicago headquarters in rural Wisconsin – became the American champion, vying with Giant for the world number one spot.

The company has not been without its troubles, particularly in the early days, and has moved a fair way from its origins as – as its name suggests – a producer of trekking or touring bikes. But it has managed to take over Schwinn's old reputation for durability and quality so that even in Britain, specialist retailers will happily recommend a Trek ahead of any number of well-known UK brands. At the same time, though, it has been more successful than most in playing to the cutting-edge crowd through ownership of such hip brands as Gary Fisher and Klein.

> *'This guy in his fifties was looking down at me like I was some jerk kid who didn't know anything.' – Gary Fisher, mountain biking pioneer, on Schwinn engineers sent out to examine the Californian craze he helped start.*

Keeping these names alive is important because it acknowledges a fact that eludes many, according to Garry Snook, founder of Performance Bikes, one of the leading US mail-order and retail suppliers of cycling equipment; that is, that cycling is not a single niche, but several.

The likes of Gary Fisher and Klein can gain from an arrangement with Trek that gives them greater marketing clout and helps make their models more competitive in terms of price by giving them access to components that – thanks to Trek's bigger buying power – become cheaper. But only so long as they are kept alive as separate 'cool' brands.

It does not matter that consumers know of the link; it even enhances the appeal of standard Trek cycles because it implies that the proprietors of the main operating company are savvy and in touch in a way that the later Schwinn executives were not. But it would be disastrous if, say, the Fisher and Klein brands became amalgamated with Trek's, because that would get the company into the trouble to which Performance's Snook alludes; it ignores the fact that the market is made up of minimarkets or niches which are populated by highly knowledge-able and discerning customers.

In other words, the Trek executives appear to recognise in a way that their counterparts at organisations such as Raleigh and the other mass-market producers do not that price is not the only differentiator. At a time when prices of even top-end cycles have fallen rapidly, it is much more important to build a rapport – or to engage with – certain groups of customers.

In this industry, as in others, the leaders seem to realise that success is not always dependent upon appealing to everybody. Indeed, the very opposite can be the case. It can be much more to do with making people feel that they are members of some exclusive club. Incidentally, the reason why so many famous brands lose their way, when some supposed marketing whizz comes along and suggests all kinds of ways of 'leveraging the brand' by spreading it to all sorts of other areas, is simply that the moment that happens, the exclusivity goes – and with it the opportunity to charge a premium price.

Chapter 2

MAKING A COMMITMENT

If you want to see the state that British business has got itself into, just look at Barclays Bank in the 1990s, especially the BZW debacle. Now, clearing banks are known for their tendency to combine a general timidity with a readiness to jump on the latest bandwagon, whether it be excessive lending to the property sector or reducing the numbers and quality of staff dealing with customers at the same time as making grand promises about service. But investment banking is supposed to be something different, something altogether bolder.

So you can imagine the thrill that went through the organisation when a new chief was hired – at great expense, even by City standards – with the goal of building a global force, powerful enough to take on the giants of Wall Street. It was sufficiently exciting – in part, at least – to overcome upset over a transplant from the City to Canary Wharf in London's Docklands, since that was the only place with enough space to house this soon-to-be colossus. But then just a few months later, the great game was over. Amid some confusion, BZW was up for sale, or parts of it were (such was the level of confusion in the immediate aftermath of the announcement, it was difficult to know for sure); the highly paid chief executive had resigned and the parent bank had authorised the payment of substantial bonuses in an effort to ensure that not too many of the only real assets of an investment bank – its people – were lured away while a buyer was sought.

What had changed in the interim? Why was a venture a good idea a few months before but not now? Well, the consolidation among the big US investment banks had continued, so presumably Barclays had had second thoughts about the scale of the task confronting it and – in classic banker's fashion – opted to cut its losses before it was in too deep. So much for vision. So much for the unstoppable abilities of Martin Taylor, the brilliant wunderkind of industry, who was not content with sorting out the bank that had audaciously hired him as chief executive but was advising the new Government too. So much, then, for Britain's new sense of worth in the wake of Tony Blair's coming to power.

But Barclays' problems did not begin and end there. It only had the somewhat idiosyncratic Taylor as its chief executive because it had, through a combination of poor lending decisions and unfocused management, got itself into such a desperate state that desperate measures were called for.

Whether or not Taylor, a former *Financial Times* journalist held in high regard on the strength of his reputedly great intellect, would have made the difference is hard to tell, since it is now apparent that he was given little chance to try. Though supposedly the head of the company, he was repeatedly stymied by his fellow directors – and not long after the ignominious retreat from investment banking he walked out.

Nor is it just banks. Take another industry at which Britain is supposed to be highly adept – agriculture and its associated businesses. Many would argue that the intensive farming techniques of which the country is so proud have played a role in the spread of the so-called mad cow disease – and so brought large parts of the industry to the brink of ruin.

Meanwhile, those involved in the milk side have shown a rare paucity of vision. With the amount of milk actually drunk in Britain on the decline, distributors such as Unigate and Hillsdown have been throwing all their energies into exploring ways of creating economies of scale and cutting costs by merging interests. But the game has moved on. People may not drink as much milk as doctors would like, but they consume vast amounts of yoghurt, fromage frais, crème fraiche and the like.

Products that were once as exotic as mangoes and pumpkins are now, like those fruits and vegetables, available on supermarket shelves throughout the land. But look closely at the labels and you will be hard-pressed to find any made by British manufacturers. Instead, supposedly sleepy continental producers dominate a market that – for all the fancy names and the fancy pricetags given the final outputs – is based on good old milk. In other words, something that British farmers produce so much of that they are hard-pressed to fetch an economic price for it could, with a little imagination, be turned into something for which they could charge much more because of its perceived extra value. As one commentator said, it is a classic case of managing decline.

To be fair, such things do not only happen in Britain. The US telecommunications giant AT&T alone has over recent years come up with a litany of acquisitions, divestments and demergers as it has lurched about in response to various management consultants' assessments. And it has paid a handsome price, too, for advice that seems to have left it no further forward than it was to start with: more than half a billion dollars in half a decade, according to the book *Dangerous Company*.

However, in Britain the combination of this US-style ruthlessness with a fundamental lack of confidence is producing the harsh results with which we are all too familiar. Stephen Roach, Morgan Stanley's chief economist and widely acknowledged as the guru of downsizing, might have attracted a lot of attention for his admission that he took the concept too far, but there still seems to be a lot of cost cutting and job shedding going on. Anybody looking for evidence to support management thinker and consultant Gary Hamel's assertion that this can become an addiction need only cast a glance at the business pages on just about any day of the results season.

Some companies – the likes of 3M and HP and a good many privately owned organisations – tend to avoid making the headlines in this way. They are also companies that do not get bogged down in 'missions' to be the greatest ever producer of this or that. And, while they have not kept sufficiently far away from consultants to have escaped the 'mission statement' disease altogether, they do not pay nearly as close attention to these often empty statements of the obvious as they do to their 'values'.

> *Only 36 per cent of organisations classified as cost-cutters between 1986 and 1991 achieved profitable growth over the next five years, according to a 1997 study by Mercer Management Consulting.*

In HP's case these are enshrined in the HP Way, a pithy document with which the two Stanford University enginering graduates Bill Hewlett and Dave Packard set out their intentions, while at 3M they are contained in the McKnight Principles – named after an early chief executive who, despite a training in accountancy, had the vision to put in train an approach to doing business that largely remains at the company today.

The HP Way has gone through various incarnations over the years, but essentially it remains unchanged, and in an in-house publication issued in 1989 it was set out as follows:

- We have trust and respect for individuals.
- We focus on a high level of achievement and contribution.
- We conduct our business with uncompromising integrity.
- We achieve our common objectives through teamwork.
- We encourage flexibility and innovation.

Meanwhile, the central part of the McKnight principles – committed to memory by many of today's executives – reads: 'Those men to whom we delegate authority and responsibility, if they are good men, are going to have ideas of their own and are going to want to do their jobs in their own way ... these are characteristics we want in men and should be encouraged ... Mistakes will be made, but ... [these] are not so serious in the long run as the mistakes management makes if it is dictatorial and undertakes to tell those under its authority exactly how they must do their job. Management that is destructively critical when mistakes are made kills initiative and it's essential that we have many people with initiative if we are to continue to grow.'

That translates into letting the scientists and customers lead the way, with managers in R&D encouraged not to say 'no'. Or, as the company's current chief executive Desi DeSimone puts it, 'innovation tells us where to go; we don't tell innovation where to go'.

If the two credos sound familiar, that is not surprising. All the management consultants in the world have not been able to improve on the gut feelings of a handful of businessmen establishing companies in the first half of this century. Though their authors could not possibly have foreseen many of the changes and technological developments with which their successors now grapple daily, employees of both companies insist that the principles provide excellent foundations as well as acting as touchstones should they be undecided about whether something is the right thing to do. At HP, for instance, it is often said that an individual or group of employees in unfamiliar circumstances will simply ask, 'What would Bill and Dave do?' At a time when many other companies are spending fortunes in time and consultancy fees on developing ethics codes, that is a powerful message.

As Professor Hamel says, cost-cutting can become an addiction. Especially when – in the short term at least – it can produce the shot in the arm to performance that the City or Wall Street is looking for. Link that to the fact that the size of many executives' pay packets is largely governed by the comparatively short-term share price performance of their companies and you need not be too much of a conspiracy theorist to see why downsizing has been so prevalent.

Indeed, it is arguable that it is not the observers seeing downsizing as aided and abetted by certain corporate practices who are cynical, but the executives themselves. After all, many do not stay around long enough to witness the end-game arrive. Instead, they are given all the credit when all-too-grateful institutions see a revival in the fortunes of their precious investments and, with reputations as brave warriors against corporate sloth and obesity enhanced, they are ushered into fresh challenges and brand new opportunities to cash in spectacular options packages through boldly slashing costs and reining in extravagances. And even when they are there when the music stops, they can find it a lot easier to get another job than most of those hapless souls they have consigned to eking out the rest of their working lives as 'consultants', 'portfolio workers' or simply unemployed or retired early.

> *When AT&T's downsizing phase was in full swing, it was joked that the company's initials would soon stand for [chief executive Robert] Allen and Two Temps. And as the company become caught further and further in a downward spiral, Allen's pay went up and up.*

Perhaps the classic case of this in recent times is Liam Strong. Hired from British Airways to turn around Sears, the ailing UK retail group built up by Sir Charles Clore, he lurched from disaster to disaster. With the exception of the flagship department store Selfridges, every business unit seemed to defy all attempts to breathe new life into them. But even when Strong gave up trying and sold units, his problems did not end. A group of sports stores sold for a song because it was felt that nothing could be done with them was quickly returned to profit by the new owner, the fast-expanding Scottish-based group Sports Division; a desperate fire sale of other units to another company backfired when the buyer – who had acquired a questionable reputation in the City – collapsed and responsibility for the shops' leases reverted to Sears; and a promise to return several hundred million pounds to overwrought investors was thrown into jeopardy when the deal that was going to provide this cash – selling the mail-order operation Freemans to Littlewoods – was referred to the competition authorities.

Finally, the board decided that everything had been tried, and little had worked. It opted to break up the company, appointed a company doctor to examine the options for the shoe business that been the company's foundation and let Strong out of his misery. No doubt relieved to be no longer the subject of countless news stories describing investors' acute disquiet with his stewardship of their funds, he kept low for a few weeks – until WorldCom, a US company of whom few British people had previously heard, made its audacious bid to ruin BT's global expansion plans by making a then world record takeover offer for telecommunications rival MCI, and appointed Strong as its UK chief.

But the retail group's inadequacies continued to be amply demonstrated after Strong left. Selfridges failed to share in the boom being enjoyed by many of its rivals, while the retail entrepreneur Philip Green sold 70 Shoe Express stores he had bought off Sears for £8m in December 1997 barely six months later for a healthy profit. He also later bought what remained of the limping company.

Now, you can argue, as some have done, that Sears' difficulties were not all down to Strong. After all, they were well advanced before his arrival. Nevertheless, he was hired – and paid a significant sum of money – to sort them out. And if his failure was not all his fault, it was a lot more his than it was the many poor souls who suffered and lost their means of support while he stumbled about. And it is a fair bet that, had everything worked out according to plan, the credit would have gone to him.

But it is less the swift rehabilitation itself than the manner of it that is truly depressing. For, though one can be considered expansionary and the other a contraction, takeovers and cost-cutting are often inextricably linked. For all the grand claims about increasing global reach and leveraging brands, most takeovers (and even the majority of those termed mergers are effectively takeovers) are not – as just about everyone involved seems to say these days – about 'one and one equalling three'. They are about economies of scale, and how, in this age of knowledge counting for more than brawn, do you achieve them? By sacking people, of course.

If companies – to borrow from George Fisher, the former Motorola chief who spent the late 1990s battling to get the venerable company of Kodak out of the mire – are 'callous' about their workforces in the general run of things, they can be doubly so when they are trying to make a takeover justify it-self. When you consider that repeated surveys from management consultants demonstrate that few of these deals work, more and more cost-cutting and job shedding are the almost inevitable results.

Given that consolidation has become so commonplace that even the companies' advisers – notably the big accounting and management consulting firms – are doing it, it is easy to see why Fisher has warned that 'the level of workplace anxiety today is at a very unhealthy level'. In fact, this anxiety is so intense that it is felt by those who are not even in the workforces concerned. Downsizing and other forms of cost-cutting that put extra strain on employees are so much the norm that eve-rybody knows somebody who has either lost their job or – sometimes worse – is battling to do the work that used to be done by two or three other people.

In such circumstances, business loses all similarities with great adventure and exciting quests for wealth, and becomes a life of drudgery. As a result, it has trouble hiring the very people it needs to prosper: the increasingly highly aware and clear-sighted students who tell every market researcher who cares to ask that they would rather work in a small organisation where they can 'make a difference' and where they have a chance of building a balanced lifestyle.

Oblivious to this, chief executives end up justifying their substantial salaries and perks by concentrating less on how it is a fair reward for all the wealth they create and more on how they need them to make up for all the hassle with which they have to cope. When business leaders gather together to mark the achievements of one of their number they quickly turn from celebration to complaint – about how they are constantly criticised and subjected to increasing rules and regulations. At such an occasion attended by the author in the late 1990s, one asserted testily that it was time he and his colleagues stood up for themselves.

He may be right. But the way to do that is through actions rather than words. In the past, the actions for which he and his counterparts have become known have too often been negative – factory closures, large-scale lay-offs, mergers, pollution disasters and, of course, what have generally been perceived to be excessive pay rises. And the words have either been dull and uninspiring or they have been let down by the actions. Not for nothing has the admonishment 'you've got to walk the talk' become a commonplace in organisations around the world.

> *Not for nothing has the admonishment 'you've got to walk the talk' become a commonplace in organisations around the world.*

THE DOWNSIDE OF DOWNSIZING

It is easy to see why downsizing – wrapped up as it has been in that other enthusiasm of the early 1990s, business process re-engineering – has attracted such a backlash. Most people commenting on it would not worry too much about the harm it is doing business in the medium term. However, they are incredibly concerned about the devastating effect it has had on not just the traditional victims of company restructurings – unskilled and semi-skilled employees – but also on people like them. For the real burden of the early 1990s downsizing craze fell on the managerial classes – making redundancy a much less pejorative term than it had been on the grounds that many of one's friends were losing their jobs 'through no fault of their own'.

In the strictest sense, that is probably true – in most cases. Downsizing has arguably attracted such public opprobrium, not just because it has brought that dreaded word 'redundancy' into the realm of the chattering classes, but because it is so obviously harmful. Other ills of the fad-driven approach to business – such as decentralisation and focus and their opposites, centralisation and diversification – are of grave concern to those whose business it is to worry about the state of industry, but they make little impression on the general public. Except to confirm the view that business is some strange place about as distant from logic as the average courtroom.

Coming as it did at a time when consultants and the business leaders who often appear to be little more than their charges were beginning to spout lofty thoughts about 'empowerment' and people being companies' greatest asset, it was bound to hit a raw nerve.

The negative impact of repeated rounds of redundancies at the same time as executives talk about employees being their 'greatest asset' has been so huge that the resulting reductions in productivity make further blood-letting inevitable.

When senior executives 'let go' another tranche of employees soon after or even as they were espousing such ideals, the result was not just cyncism about the latest contributions to a concept that is known in parts of North America as the 'Bohica effect', for 'bend over, here it comes again'. It also threw into question everything that such managers said or did.

In other words, the negative impact was so huge that – as anybody who put any store at all by the idea that people are more productive if they are well motivated and basically happy would readily conclude – the organisations concerned were bound to have to go through another round of blood-letting – simply because, barring miracles, the next quarter's results would be bound to be worse than those in the previous period.

It is largely for this reason that Britain's Royal Society for the Encouragement of Arts, Manufactures and Commerce ran into so much flak when in the early 1990s it published its interim version of the *Tomorrow's Company* report. Not only was the thinking in that early document rather more 'flaky' and 'do-gooding' than that later espoused by the centre that it spawned, but some of the companies that signed up for the exercise were going through fairly dramatic job-cutting programmes at the time. Of course, as one chief executive concerned explained, the cuts he was pushing through were necessary for structural reasons.

When they were completed, he and his colleagues would be in a position to put into practice the ideas they had supported. It hardly needs to be said that when the strong pound combined with fears of a return to recession in the late 1990s, many of those same companies found that their first reaction was to reach for the jobs axe.

But it could hardly have softened the blow for those valuable assets deemed surplus to requirements to know that they were being fired for reasons that had to do with impossible-to-withstand changes going on in individual industries rather than a mere downturn. Nor could it have much heartened those left behind to realise that there was not necessarily much that they could do about avoiding the same fate. After all, one of the initiatives that so obviously backfired was the repeated insistence on the part of senior executives, and their personnel or human resources advisers, that those losing their jobs were not being singled out. It was not their fault, they said, as if these people just happened to have been in the wrong place at the wrong time. If that is not a recipe for encouraging employees to give up and wait for the inevitable next round of redundancies, it is hard to know what is.

Equally predictable was the fact that the employees with the most to offer and whom – in normal circumstances – an organisation would least want to lose would respond to such a situation by either looking for opportunities elsewhere or – as a result of this confidence in their ability to find work – put themselves in a position whereby they figured in the next redundancy round; either by directly applying for whatever package was on offer or by behaving in such a way that they were deemed to have lost what usefulness they previously had.

To see the potential for chaos created by generous voluntary redundancy programmes, one only has to look at BT. The company's various high-profile television advertisement campaigns – themselves capable of being viewed as a cynical attempt to keep competitors out of its market by raising the barriers to entry – may promote a cuddly image, but within the organisation the struggle to transform itself from an old-fashioned nationalised industry into a modern commercial giant has been tough. (Not least because for much of its life the company has had to fend off press comments about its annual telephone-number-size profits – usually with the somewhat lame excuses that the numbers are not as big as they look and, anyway, such funds will be needed to help survive the hard times ahead.)

And the thwarting of the company's global ambitions through WorldCom's swoop for would-be partner MCI has done nothing to lighten the mood. Even before this hugely ambitious, but crucially important deal distracted management attention, insiders talked of wave after wave of often contradictory management initiatives. Always overhanging the scene has been the spectre of further rounds of job cuts. According to the book *Trust and Transition* by Peter Herriot, Wendy Hirsh and Peter Reilly, the company saw the size of its workforce nearly halve between 1990 and 1996, with the staff headcount reduced from 245,000 to 134,000.

But disastrous as such situations are, there is no escaping the fact that millions of managers and their predecessors at BT and far beyond had helped create them for themselves through the things they did and did not do in the years leading up to the early 1990s, when fierce recession and the Gulf crisis conspired to blow a chill wind through just about every industry you can name.

There is little doubt that in the 'go-go years' of the 1980s, people in all kinds of businesses were doing too well. They were paying themselves too much for doing work that was often not especially clever nor, in all honesty, that time-consuming.

> *They were paying themselves too much for doing work that was often not especially clever nor, in all honesty, that time-consuming.*

Britain, the USA, Japan and other parts of the industrialised world enjoyed a boom that stretched even beyond the Crash of 1987, but on the whole they did not use it to deal with things that they must have known had not been fixed.

In both Britain and the USA, for instance, the car industry was still in some trouble. While Detroit's dinosaurs found themselves at the mercy of the increasingly confident Japanese companies such as Honda and Toyota, the City's yuppies did not splash out their money on Jags and Rollers; they opted for Porsches and transformed a previously little known marque called BMW into an international symbol of affluence – paving the way, incidentally, for the German manufacturer's takeover of the remnants of the British car industry.

Such circumstances were made for the likes of Albert Dunlap, a group of corporate hard men who have made a significant contribution to the downsizing trend that hit both sides of the Atlantic in the early 1990s. Consultant Larry Reynolds, in his book 'The Trust Effect', relates that in the first three years of the Clinton presidency AT&T and IBM each laid off 120,000 people, General Motors 100,000, Boeing 60,000 and Sears Roebuck 50,000.

In June 1998, Dunlap – known as 'Rambo in Pinstripes' or 'Chainsaw Al' – received his comeuppance when the independent directors of the ailing kitchen products group Sunbeam forced him out over the company's weak performance in the previous few months. Much fun has been had with the fact that Dunlap was even more the author of his own misfortune than is usually the case in these situations because his policy of forcing outside directors to buy stock and to be paid in it made them acutely aware of his failings.

However, this setback does not mask the untold damage he – and others like him – have over the years done not just to individual organisations and employees but also to business in general.

Of course, not everybody sees it that way. In the cover story of the 15 January 1996 issue of *Business Week*, Wayne Sanders, chairman of Kimberley-Clark, the company with which Dunlap's Scott Paper had then just concluded a $9.4 billion merger, is quoted as saying, 'he has been a wake-up call to a lot of CEOs, and he has been good for American business'. Dunlap himself – who walked away from the deal with nearly $100 million in salary, bonus, stock gains and other perks – is proud of what he calls 'one of the most successful, quickest turnarounds ever.'

In his 20-month stint at the company, Scott's stock rose 225 per cent, adding $6.3 billion to the value of the company, while the earnings figures for the quarter leading up to the December 1995 deal were a record $155.4 million, far ahead of Wall Street's expectations.

However, while the performance made the previously little-known chief executive into a star in great demand as a business school speaker, even at the time of the deal plenty of people suggested that Scott was not in such good shape as Dunlap claimed. In a precursor to the battle between profit fans and those who favour expanding market share that is discussed in a later chapter of this book, they say that when Dunlap was reporting record profits and boosting returns for investors, the company's share of certain key markets was falling.

And the blame for that, say former executives quoted by *BusinessWeek*, lays at least partly with Dunlap's penchant for cutting muscle along with the fat. During his brief tenure, he not only eliminated 11,000 jobs – 71 per cent of headquarters staff, 50 per cent of the managers and 20 per cent of hourly workers – he dramatically cut spending on research and development and on training – cuts that many predicted would make it hard for Kimberly to recoup the half a billion dollars or so in synergies and cost reductions expected by analysts at the time of the deal.

Much the same sort of policies have been followed at such British companies as Hanson, by common consent, the conglomerate's conglomerate until the stock market's turn against such creatures led it to break itself up in the mid-1990s, and BTR.

The latter adopted the 'selling-off-the-family silver' route in an attempt to keep itself going. Ian Strachan, the chief executive brought in to sort out a company that had begun to ail almost as soon as its authoritarian creator Owen Green had stepped down, characterised such deals as an effort to give the sprawling organisation a focus. But others saw the departure of Slazenger and other notable businesses as getting rid of the only bits that were worth anything.

This made the merger with Siebe, announced in the autumn of 1998, something of a coup. However, it also hinted at a worrying loss of faith on the part of Siebe, which – though latterly run by an American – was the beacon of Britain's struggling engineering sector. True, Siebe had always gone in for mergers and acquisitions, but in taking on an organisation like BTR, which had jettisoned most of its jewels on its way down, it was taking a big risk in the name of that sorry quest to be 'the world's biggest' – in this case, controls company.

Dunlap, a West Point graduate and former paratrooper, seems to have revelled in making the metaphors real and bringing a warlike attitude to the boardroom. His autobiography, *Mean Business: How I Save Bad Companies and Make Good Companies Great*, sets out his approach in typically uncompromising style. 'Business is simple, remarkably simple' and 'You're not in business to be liked. Neither am I. We're here to succeed. If you want a friend, get a dog.' are probably his most famous statements.

But his credo extends a little further, taking in such principles as the most important person in the organisation is far and away the shareholder; reward leadership and outstanding performance at every level of the organisation – the corollary being that running a major corporation warrants just about any amount of money; firing lots of people is justified on the basis that it can be the only way of keeping the rest of the workforce in employment; and 'You can outsource just about anything today.'

> *Firing lots of people is justified on the basis that it can be the only way of keeping the rest of the workforce in employment.*

In case you are wondering why a US slasher and burner is getting so much attention, take note of the fact that he really hit his stride when in the employ of a British company. His reputation had begun to grow in the early 1980s, when he sorted out the troubled Lily Tulip company by firing half of the headquarters staff and a quarter of salaried employees. But it was when he hooked up with the late Sir James Goldsmith, no pussycat himself, to help turn around his US operations that he came into his own. It was in this period that he won the 'Chainsaw' moniker after a Goldsmith friend admired his ability to cut the fat from stodgy companies.

After that came a two-year stint with the television and magazine empire owned by Australian billionaire Kerry Packer. Dunlap was in fact in his late 50s and in retirement when the call came from Scott.

Though the board apparently expected swift action and implementation of things that former executives claim had been planned for sometime before the tough guy's appearance, they must have got more than they bargained for. According to *Business Week*, he 'brought a leveraged buy-out mind-set to Scott: slashing expenses, ditching assets and paring debt'.

In keeping with that approach, many insiders began to suspect that, for all his protestations that he was out to reinvest in the business and create a vision for the future, his real interest was in selling out.

At Sunbeam, of course, he did not get the chance to sell. Commentators queued up to kick this snarling dog when he was down. Richard Lambert, editor of the *Financial Times*, was among the leaders, pointing out that this was a man who for most of his career was 'a hired rottweiler' employed by Goldsmith and Packer to do their toughest jobs 'and then popped back in his kennel with a hunk of meat and a few million dollars'. His fall, he added, 'sent a happy glow around the business world'.

But, while getting his few kicks in, Lambert does not fall for the line that, as he puts it, 'in the caring, sharing 1990s, Chainsaw Al's approach to management has gone the way of *Tyrannosaurus rex*'. Though he says that Dunlap apparently did not realise that times had changed and that there was a growing sense in the USA that the rewards of success needed to be shared more widely, he points to two other factors that are unconnected with this phenomenon. The first was believing his own publicity. The second was disregarding his rule about the fundamental importance of the shareholders. By presiding over a fall in the share price he gave the independent directors, who had been required to buy substantial amounts of stock and to take their pay in shares, plenty of reason to force him out.

Satisfying as this may have been to many people – particularly the thousands that he fired over the years – it does not actually advance things much beyond the 'he who lives by the sword, dies by the sword' arguments. For the fundamental problem with Dunlap's approach is that – outrageous and overly provocative as some of his language is – the nub of the policy is not unique to him. Executives throughout the Anglo-Saxon business world are running hundreds and hundreds of companies by what are essentially the same rules.

Lambert, after all, argues in his article that the economic success being enjoyed by the USA in the late 1990s owed something to Dunlap and his kind over the previous decade and a half. Senior managers have been shaken out of complacency and self-indulgence, while companies have cut costs and focused on their basic businesses. 'Other nations have lagged behind and need this treatment', he writes.

But do they? Warren Bennis, a US academic who is one of the most thoughtful writers on management in general and leadership in particular, does not think so. In fact, he feels that the man and his book could prove highly valuable, albeit in an unintended way.

In a review of *Mean Business*, Bennis, under the heading 'The Neanderthal in the Corner Office', writes: 'Dunlap seems to have proudly adopted the philosophies of Attila the Hun and the Mafia Manager' before concluding that he is 'truly grateful to Chainsaw Al for clarifying what has gone so wrong with so many of our nation's corporations'.

Since the US way of business is held in such awe in Britain, by extension, Dunlap – albeit on a much larger scaale – also demonstrates the failings of this approach on this side of the water. Building products companies such as Rugby and Blue Circle as well as other grand old names such as Pilkington and ICI are typical of companies that cannot get off the cost-cutting roundabout. As one management writer said, the biggest predictor of a company making job cuts this year is that they did so last year.

> *The biggest predictor of a company making job cuts this year is that they did so last year.*

It is no wonder that many people outside business – as well as those already operating in this sort of way – see the simplistic 'take no prisoners' attitude of Dunlap and his various followers as typical of business – in much the same way that they are inclined to see *Wall Street*'s Gordon Gekko as the epitome of an investment banker and therefore justification of all their misgivings.

Having noted that Dunlap is of the shareholders'-interests-are-paramount school, Bennis adds: 'By showing us what happens when a single, ruthless individual wields too much corporate power, he teaches a contrary lesson. Al, you and your shareholders are only part of the equation. We are all in this together.'

THE TYRANNY OF FADS

The Individualized Corporation, by Sumatra Ghoshal of London Business School and Christopher Bartlett of Harvard, is one of a growing group of books arguing that the old corporate model with which many managers and other employees have grown up is outmoded. Just as it has become accepted that the character of work has changed so that it no longer fits the common idea of a lifetime of regular weeks' work for a single employer, so it is increasingly widely assumed that the organisation for which most people do that work is taking on a new aspect.

Convincing as all this seems – especially if you are one of those overworked managers dragging more and more work home from the office (if not physically then via the wonders of modern communications technology) – there must be at least a suspicion among the more cynical that all this could be a fad, just like so many much-heralded new approaches of the past. After all, recent years alone have seen the likes of customer service, quality, learning and knowledge all accorded mythical status – only for new groups of consultants and scholars to come along and put holes in them.

But that seems to be the way of business. Insights are hyped up into full-blown theories that then become marketed as *the* answer to all business problems of the time. Then setbacks occur – sometimes causing the original proponents, as was the case with re-engineering, to rush to be the first to point out the limitations of the original theory or to put forward a refinement.

Often, the problems arise from the fact that it is one thing for senior executives to state that they are going to do something and quite another for them to achieve it.

Take innovation. In the late 1990s, it became a mantra for businesses everywhere. Never mind that being innovative is like motherhood, especially in the digital age. Everybody had to mention innovation as often as possible in all their corporate communications. After all, the management gurus were seemingly united in their belief that only the most innovative organisations could be assured of success.

Yet research published in mid-1998 by the Confederation of British Industry showed UK industry defying calls to innovate for future success by continuing to reduce expenditure in this area. The 1998 Innovation Trends Survey, sponsored by NatWest Innovation and Growth Unit and the UK arm of 3M, revealed that manufacturing companies spent 4.9 per cent of turnover on innovation in 1997, down from 5.9 per cent the previous year and from the 1994 peak of 6.7 per cent. The figures also showed that the median level was 2.1 per cent of turnover, suggesting that many firms only spend modest amounts in this area.

Spending by non-manufacturers dropped even more dramatically – to 5.4 per cent of turnover, compared with 11.8 per cent in 1996. Though the researchers point out that this may be attributable to a change in the type of companies from 1996, the trend remains – year-on-year declines since the high levels of 1994.

The survey took a broad approach to innovation – going beyond strict research and development and exploitation of new technologies to look at process innovation, supply chain integration and broad innovation strategies, where companies committed to innovation on R&D, marketing, training and capital investment.

The decline in UK spending across this range of activities comes despite the fact that management consultancies and gurus, such as Gary Hamel, are constantly warning companies that at a time of low inflation the only way for them to grow is to innovate – by launching new products, improving service and conducting their business in different ways.

As Adair Turner, director-general of the CBI, said: 'The results should set off alarm bells for British business. In a rapidly changing world we need to innovate to survive, yet the figures suggest that the lessons of the past have not yet been learned.'

> *'In a rapidly changing world we need to innovate to survive, yet the figures suggest that the lessons of the past have not yet been learned.' – Adair Turner of the CBI.*

One person who would not be surprised by such findings is Richard Pascale, the noted business school academic, author and consultant. Several years ago, he published in one of his books a chart plotting the shelf lives of some of the best-known fads. So compelling was the case when it was set down like that it has become the received wisdom among cynics everywhere that management is often about little more than understanding the latest fads and their attendant buzzwords.

As Pascale himself admits, somewhat wearily and only half tongue-in-cheek, being anti-fads has become a fad in itself. Yet even those who decry the fads find the allure of the handful of simple principles, techniques or tools irresistible. Hence, the books that start off by denouncing just about all that has gone on in the past only to set out their own prescriptions for success.

Essentially, the real problem with management theories is that so many of them are – superficially at least – plausible. Take, for example, the recent enthusiasm for growth and innovation. That seems so obvious, especially at a time of low inflation, that it is almost accorded the famous 'motherhood and apple pie' status. After all, as the consultants never tire of saying, 'no company ever shrank to greatness'.

But then along comes a line of thinking that suggests that in going all-out for growth, business is ignoring many of the lessons of the 1980s, when a good many companies grew their way to oblivion. The trick is to go for the 'right kind of growth'.

No matter that if there is generally reckoned to a single guiding principle behind success in business it is probably gaining market share. Become market leader or, at a pinch, the second-placed company in your market, and you cannot go wrong, say pundits and managers alike.

This is, after all, the thinking behind many of the mergers of the late 1990s mergers and acquisitions boom. For example, those responsible for creating that accounting behemoth PricewaterhouseCoopers (PwC), as well as those that did not end up linking up after all, have put great store by being 'the world's biggest professional services firm'. Even companies that have not hit the acquisition trail put such store by market share that they trumpet their impressive positions in their various markets throughout their annual reports. Aiming to be 'number one' is reckoned to be such a self-evidently grand strategy that questioning it is seen as naive in the extreme. Get lots of revenue and the profits will inevitably follow, not least because of the resulting economies of scale, goes the argument.

However, while this sort of approach may have worked for Lord Weinstock when he was building up GEC, it does not seem as powerful today as many merger partners would have you believe. Indeed, some of PwC's rivals in the professional services field are taking the view that there are some clients that they would rather not have, and there is a growing school of thought that believes that 'market share is dead'.

As Adrian Slywotzky and David Morrison of Mercer Management Consulting point out in their book *The Profit Zone*, some disturbing examples have begun to 'subvert the widespread faith in market share as the ultimate goal and guarantor of business success'. Such well-known US companies as IBM, Digital Equipment, General Motors, Ford, Kodak and Sears Roebuck have all achieved leading market share positions and yet seen their profitability, and hence their share values, eroded during the 1980s.

Some of these organisations have recovered of late, but the authors attribute that recovery at least in part to focusing on profit rather than just market share. In short, they have realised that, though market share might have been 'the grand old metric, the guiding light, the compass of the product-centric age', it is no longer.

The thoughtful manager will probably have come to this conclusion, simply by looking around and seeing how many companies – particularly in the high-tech arena – have made healthy profits just by operating effectively in niches. But it is quite another thing for him or her to work out a way of turning a company that has hitherto been focused on market share into one that concentrates on profitability.

Slywotzky and Morrison argue that achieving this is dependent on understanding the concept of 'no-profit zones', or the 'black holes of the business universe'. These increasingly common phenomena come in various forms – they can be part of the value chain – for example distribution in computers; they can be customer segments – i.e. consistent bad debtors, if you are a utility, or those who remain steadfastly in the black and carry out few transactions if you are a bank; they can be entire industries – for example, environmental remediation; or they can be entire business models, such as the integrated steel mills that have been bested by the 'mini-mills'.

Once this concept is clear, the theory goes, managers will be able to identify 'profit zones', or those sorts of activities that are worthy of their attention on the grounds that they – unlike market share per se – are likely to produce profit.

Never mind that this sounds pretty much like the old focus on profits that we were being encouraged to be so dismissive of only a short while later. What is really notable is how the same old suspects keep cropping up to give the theory credence. Consequently, we have Jack Welch of General Electric of the USA, former Coca-Cola chief executive Roberto Goizueta and Michael Eisner of Disney all lined up to demonstrate how they used this sort of thinking to create value for their organisations. Now, they may well have done so, but – since we know, from loads of other books and articles, that they have also embraced many other techniques – how can we know how much of their success is attributable to this latest approach?

At Disney, for example, we are told how Eisner has used merchandise licensing – in the authors' words – to knit the entire Disney empire together. Mickey Mouse, the Lion King and other characters are repeatedly pressed into action in order to provide a common link between films, theme parks, theme park hotels, video sales and even clothes sales. There is little risk of somebody, particularly a child, just seeing a film or visiting a theme park. It is little wonder that Slywotzky and Morrison reckon Disney is able to take as much as 75 per cent of a family's holiday spend – by owning the hotel, the theme park, the restaurants, the merchandise. But this is a pretty unique example. Not many organisations are in such a strong position to help patrons part with their hard-earned cash.

If this is not the only way of going about achieving the 'right kind of growth', it is also true that there are a lot more components to the success of these august organisations. Disney and Coca-Cola, obviously, have put a lot of store by brand, while

GE has proven adept at adapting to changing times and venturing into previously unknown areas, notably financing via the hugely successful GE Capital, in the search for sustainable success.

Similarly, the success of Texas-based computer company Dell – cited in support of the similar 'profit pool' theory put forward by Bain & Co – is down to a lot more than returning to its direct selling roots in the search for profitable customers. Sure, that has helped. But – just as with the upstart direct-selling financial services organisations that it so closely resembles – the prosperity is just as likely to be a product of such factors as adaptability, competitive pricing enabled by lower costs and the drive of its founders.

Indeed, in explaining how the company arrived at the decision to abandon retailing, Bain partners Orit Gadiesh and James Gilbert demonstrate a characteristic of Dell's executives that is probably not shared by all their rivals: a willingness to analyse the data. Only by doing that in the detail that they did could they have had any inkling of who their most profitable customers were. For a comparison, just look at how most banks, despite investing millions in information technology, have only the slightest idea of who their customers are.

The point is that the companies that get into trouble do not seem to be savvy enough to realise that there is not, and never will be, a short cut to success. Executives are not nearly wary enough of those – gurus, consultants and the rest – who point to successful companies and say they got there just by doing this or that.

Gurus always talk in absolutes – because they understand publishing and the media well enough to know that it is the simple, all-encompassing statements (which preferably confound much that has gone before) that gain attention, while well-considered arguments barely make it out of the academic journals. The caveats tend to come later, when companies are running into trouble implementing these ideas.

This happened most graphically with the enthusiasm for re-engineering, which was, admittedly, at least partly blown off course by the onset of a deep recession in most of the economies where organisations were seeking to reintroduce it. But there were enough inherent problems for the originators to put their hands up and say that they got parts wrong, or at least had not been clear enough about the applications for companies to be able to have a painless implementation period.

Management theories can be extremely useful in providing fresh insights. Indeed, the greatest value that consultants have is in bringing new thinking to people who, despite their best efforts, are often so close to problems that they cannot see solutions. Accordingly, senior executives of highly successful and much-admired companies will happily endorse books, for the simple reason that they are open-minded enough to know that they do not have all the answers themselves. But this willingness to try out new thinking does not mean that they think these books provide answers.

Eileen Shapiro, in her book *Fad Surfing in the Boardroom*, says that the key is to 'review the fads that may provide you with new insights, learn from them, adapt them as seems appropriate in your best judgement, and then accept with enthusiasm the risks that are part and parcel of the courage to manage'.

Indeed, the subtitle of her book makes it clear that she believes managers need to 'reclaim the courage to manage in the age of instant answers'. This does not mean ignoring all the fads. As has already been pointed out, many of the world's most successful companies are as aware of which theories and techniques are in vogue as the perennial underachievers; it is just that they have the self-confidence required to pick and choose among them.

> *Managers need to 'reclaim the courage to manage in the age of instant answers', says author Eileen Shapiro.*

Likening management to being a pilot, Shapiro says that it is about 'assessing situations, setting an overall course or focus, thinking through options, developing plans, taking action, learning, modifying plans, learning more and continuing to go forward.' Though none of this is especially new, life has been made more complex for the modern manager by 'the sheer number of techniques proposed for meeting these needs – and positioned, in many cases, as panaceas that obviate the need to think as long as the formula is followed.'

Moreover, because there are so many programmes promoted with such heavy marketing, 'the temptation to operate on autopilot is ever-present'. This leads to two related problems. First, managers can lose the confidence to make their own decisions and so increasingly rely on the assistance of the ever-ready consultants. Second, organisations become subjected to so many initiatives that they become paralysed. Even programmes that have huge potential on their own can be rendered valueless if the people charged with implementing them have seen so many previous schemes that they lack the necessary enthusiasm to carry out the job.

Author and journalist John Case, in his book *The Open-Book Management Experience*, explains how, where once corporate managers could announce an initiative and expect that most people would at least give it the benefit of the doubt, these days 'change initiatives run smack into the Dilbert phenomenon'. Fifteen years of managerial fads and buzzwords mean that 'about the best reactions they can expect are snickers around the water cooler and a rash of Dilbert cartoons tacked anonymously on bulletin boards.'

Alternatively, an approach can gain a lot of attention – as happened with Ricardo Semler's experiments with empowerment (chronicled in his book *Maverick*) in the mid-1990s – only to lose ground as some other idea comes along. It is not that Semler's ideas were suddenly found to be worthless – though they were perhaps not applicable to every business situation – nor is it to say that 'knowledge management', 'learning organisations' and the like are so much better. In fact, there is a good deal of Semler's approach in the so-called Open Book Management, which – as its name suggests – involves helping employees to manage better on their own by letting them know the whole picture, rather than just what management has felt they needed to learn.

No, it is just that there is so much going on and managers have been encouraged by gurus and consultancies to believe that it is their misfortune to find themselves striving to manage at the most turbulent and altogether challenging time known to man. Accordingly, they are jumpy and prone to pick up on all the latest things in the hope that they will provide answers.

To return to the current area of conflict, there is an encouraging sign in a theory that basically says that not all business is good business: that, in moving yet another step away from the 'take it or leave it' school of business, successful companies are realising that – even though going for growth is probably more sustainable than cost cutting – what really matters is not products but customers.

Once companies really focus on customers they realise that they cannot possibly serve all of them equally. The latest thinking calls for them quite callously to drop those not deemed profitable enough. A more positive and forward-thinking attitude might put this in terms of building lasting relationships with those customers that they really want.

The trouble, of course, is that some companies will adhere to this principle, as they have for some time, but others will abandon it for some other convincing-sounding notion that has probably, by the time you read this, already come along.

Chapter 3

PURPOSE IN A TURBULENT WORLD

For those with a downer on business, the takeover deal has always seemed especially pernicious. It is a mechanism that is fundamental to the working of the capital markets in that it is the means by which capital is taken away from those who are not felt to be doing a good job with it and transferred to those who are thought likely to do better. But in so doing, it conjures up many of the negative images of the business world – notably job losses and plant closures associated with the cost savings that have long been the greatest justification for such deals.

Now that repeated research has indicated that few deals produce a return on the premium above the market value that companies traditionally have to pay in order to persuade the incumbent management to give up, takeover deals have increasingly been replaced by agreed mergers. Since increasingly numbers of deals involve large entities, such an approach also has an advantage in helping to smooth the passage through competition proceedings.

Nevertheless, the same thinking – or lack of it – is often at work. To put it bluntly, when a company cannot think of a new line to pursue or is being given a hard time by a competitor, its management's thoughts tend towards merger – either with a competitor if it is small, so effectively taking it out, or with another established player that is having trouble facing up to the new reality, on the basis that their sheer size will scare off the opposition or at least give them a better chance of hanging on for a while in the absence of new ideas.

Fittingly, given that the pressure to consolidate typically comes from financial types worried either about the return on their investments or about their need for fees from deals, financial services organisations have been showing an especial keenness in this regard. During a spate of such deals in the spring of 1998, the ubiquitous management guru Gary Hamel wrote an opinion piece in the *Financial Times* attacking the logic behind them. Concentrating on the then just announced link-up between Citicorp, the large US banking group headed by John Reed, and Travelers Group, the hodge-podge of financial services operations built up by Sandy Weill, he questioned the validity of the 'two tired ideas' of bulk and breadth.

'Citicorp and Travelers are certainly not resource constrained, but where are the big new ideas behind the big new company?' he wrote. Long an enemy of cost-cutting, he argued that the success of such 'heretics' or 'revolutionaries' as Southwest Airlines, the coffee shop chain Starbucks, BT's nemesis WorldCom, Dell Computer and the financial broker Charles Schwab underscored 'a fundamental reality of the new economy' that innovation is more important than size.

His point that the truth had somehow become lost in the hype surrounding the escalating size of mergers is nowhere better demonstrated than by the fact that even the Bank of England at much the same time acknowledged that there would be more mergers in the financial sector. And this from an organisation whose former deputy governor, Howard Davies, had

been among the most vocal opponents of the planned accountancy mergers that created in PricewaterhouseCoopers 'the
world's biggest professional services firm'.

But why – apart from Professor Hamel – has there been such
widespread agreement on this phenomenon? The urge to merge
seems to be challengeable on a number of counts. Not least is
the fact that, just as it is often said that consolidation into 'national champions', 'key players', call them what you will, is
inevitable, so it is said to the point of tedium that a good proportion of the wealth and job creation in developed economies
such as Britain and the USA is down to small and medium-
sized companies that have entered their respective markets in
recent years.

In other words, any problems that Barclays
might have are less to do with the annoying
presence of NatWest than with the arrival of
new entrants, such as Virgin or the various
direct sellers of financial services. Through
their small size and entrepreneurial approach
they are better able to respond to the needs of
an ever more sophisticated and demanding
customer base. It is difficult to see how getting bigger is going to help an organisation in this way.

> *Any problems that Barclays might have are less to do with the annoying presence of NatWest than with the arrival of new entrants, such as Virgin or the various direct sellers of financial services.*

Admittedly, the large accountancy firms have not been subjected to competition from more agile competitors in the same
way as the high street banks. The sheer scale and complexity
of the work they do mean that only a few of the very largest
international firms compete among each other for assignments.
But there is a clear danger that by getting so much bigger –
PwC boasts that it will be the world's 61st largest employer
with something like 135,000 staff – both staff and clients will
fall away out of conviction that their interests are not best served
by hanging around.

For the moment, this amalgamation of Price Waterhouse and
Coopers & Lybrand claims it remains wedded to serving clients

that, while growing, are not yet at the multinational stage. But how are partners serving such clients going to collect the fees that will be deemed appropriate by what is almost certain to be a more tightly managed operation? Likewise, are not budding entrepreneurs likely to be put off appointing this mega firm for fear that, even if they can afford the fees, they will get little attention from the firm's best people?

The senior partners of the so-called second-tier firms are so convinced that the latter will happen that they are marshalling their forces in readiness – and among the steps they are taking is attempting to wrest away dissatisfied partners from the large entities.

Peter Smith, the former Coopers chief who became UK senior partner of the new firm, and his erstwhile PW counterpart Ian Brindle, who took on the chairmanship, have repeatedly asserted that they needed to go down this route because they were constrained from growing. Yet, as pointed out by Linda Yates, chief executive of Strategos, the California-based management consultancy founded by Professor Hamel, why does a firm think it can only grow by merging? Is it not the received wisdom that it is easier to expand off a small base than off a larger one?

The accountancy firm executives also claim that the cost of expanding into the emerging economies, seen as such a dead cert for future riches that (like many of their clients) they cannot get there fast enough, is so horrendous that it can only be borne by linking up with another party. But senior managers at Arthur Andersen, the accountancy firm that knows more than most about worldwide growth (as well as a fair bit about the perils of size, as a result of its bitter dispute with Andersen Consulting), insist that the biggest factor in the costs of the information technology that PwC and – until they pulled out of merging – KPMG and Ernst & Young kept talking about is people. So merging will increase costs in this area rather than reduce them.

Then there are the not-insignificant diseconomies of scale. If it is generaly reckoned that partnerships are hard to manage, then imagine how easy it is to run the world's largest professional services firm, even with a powerful international executive.

Even before the deal was formally cleared by the European authorities, Coopers launched a recruitment campaign bolstered by advertising on the grounds that the combined firm around the world would need to find a thousand new faces a week to meet projected rates of expansion. Even if the much talked-about skills shortages enabled it to find people of the right calibre, just handling such numbers and imbuing in them any sense of what this new entity would be about would be a heavy management task. When challenged on this, a spokesperson explained that many human resources professionals would be among those taken on.

Perhaps the most compelling argument against all this activity is the likely attitude of clients and customers. There might be a sound logic behind building up an operation so comprehensive in what it offers that anybody needing anything vaguely financial goes to one or other of your outlets, but that does not make sufficient allowance for human beings' reluctance to put all their eggs in one basket.

The case against this view is even more powerful in professional services. Accountancy firms, having already made great headway in the lucrative area of management consultancy, are now targeting legal services. Andersen has been the most successful, though its original venture, Garretts, is reckoned to have lost its way a little and by the end of 1998 had failed to pick up the leading City firm it wanted. But the other leading firms mostly have legal operations of various kinds.

A sensible move away from the 'commodity product' of audit and towards an area where there is more perceived value, you might think. But only up to a point. Clients are now so sophisticated that they rarely give all their legal work to one firm of lawyers, let alone entrust it to the legal operation of an accountancy firm that also does audit or other work for it.

As Professor Hamel has pointed out, 'cross-selling works only when what is being sold really is a collection of the best. In today's world of sophisticated, informed customers, even great products will not tug mediocre ones along with them.'

> *Cross-selling works only when what is being sold really is a collection of the best. In today's world of sophisticated, informed customers, even great products will not tug mediocre ones along with them, says Gary Hamel.*

So, if mergers do not succeed on the basis of economies of scale or cross-selling, what does drive them? To hear the analysts, you would think that it was all the 'value' that is suddenly expected to be released when two companies announce that they are getting together. However, to judge from those deals that break down even where large amounts of shareholder value are supposedly going to be produced, this is not all that important a factor.

As times goes on, it seems less and less cynical to believe that the overriding drive behind mergers is personal ego. Analysts and other commentators these days increasingly talk of the chances of personality clashes when assessing deals and many reckon – only partly tongue in cheek – that the chances of a deal going all the way are increased where the respective chief executives are not of the same generation: that way the elder can quite reasonably take on the chairman's role, leaving the younger and usually more dynamic one to lead the new company forward.

SHAREHOLDER VALUE AND OTHER VALUES

All executives these days seem to pepper their conversation with some form of the words 'creating shareholder value'. Where once they would talk a lot about price/earnings ratios and earnings per share, now they, along with the analysts, increasingly acknowledge the importance of creating value for the owners of companies.

On the face of it, this is a beneficial move – especially since many managers have developed the habit of inserting that magic word 'sustainable' into the phrase. Such a focus is hardly surprising. Deep down, boards have always known that their role is to produce better-than-average returns for investors. After all, if they do not, they feel the full weight of market forces – usually in the form of a takeover bid.

However, as Mark Scott, the former operations director of the marketing and advertising group WPP, points out, until recently executives did not think too much about owners. 'Often the unspoken objective was to give the top managers a gentle and elegant ride, regardless of what this implied for the performance of the profit line,' he writes in his book *Value Drivers*.

Though such attitudes remain in isolated pockets, the upheavals since the 1980s boom came to an abrupt end have brought into being an approach that is at once more focused and wider ranging. On the one hand, the corporate governance debate initiated by the Cadbury Committee has reminded boards of their stewardship role; on the other, the increasing acceptance of both the 'balanced scorecard' and the 'stakeholder' concepts means that it is acknowledged that sustained value creation is only possible if attention is paid to a variety of factors. Indeed, the spur to the setting up of the Cadbury Committee – the spate of corporate collapses at the end of the 1980s – has also been behind the re-examination of performance measurement techniques.

But in their rush to come up with formulae for measuring shareholder value creation, there is surely a danger that the various accounting and consulting firms active in this area will end up producing the same kind of prescriptive list of factors that they are supposedly seeking to avoid. Though it is tempting to believe that consultancies adopt this sort of approach be-cause, like the gurus and their oversimplified books, they think it is making things more accessible to hapless managers, it is hard to shake off the notion that this is in fact yet another triumph of marketing over substance, with every operator want-ing to get their formula in on the act before things move on.

Much of the explanation for this enthusiasm lies in the de-sire to come up with a corrective to all the excesses of past years – as well as a natural concern, if not to ensure that it goes on for ever, at least to try to prolong the boom for as long as possible.

Consequently, the Price Waterhouse Financial & Cost Man-agement Team produced a book, *CFO, Architect of the Cor-poration's Future*, that explains how the likes of Maxwell Com-munications and Coloroll provide 'spectacular illustrations' of the shortcomings of EPS, in particular. Both those companies collapsed at the cusp of the 1980s and 1990s, despite high re-ported profits and revenues looking good, while Polly Peck reported profits of £161 million, a 70 per cent growth in earn-ings on the previous year, only days before falling to earth.

Combined with the realisation that, at a time when business is becoming increasingly international, the subjectivity of ac-counting conventions means that EPS calculations for a single company in a single year can vary from country to country, such examples have led institutional investors to move away from accounting-based evaluation methods like EPS, return on equity and return on investment to economic techniques based on cash flow. With business becoming much more global, they want to avoid anomalies like that which occurred when the German industrial company Daimler-Benz listed on the New York Stock Exchange in 1993. What looked a highly profit-able concern under German accounting rules appeared to turn into a heavy loss maker when US principles were applied.

The growing tendency for institutional fund managers to assess their investments around the world according to shareholder value techniques is leading more and more companies to fall into line. As usual, the tidal wave began in the USA, but such well-focused UK groups as Boots and Lloyds TSB have signed up to join such renowned value creators as Coca-Cola and General Electric.

> *As usual, the tidal wave began in the USA, but such well-focused UK groups as Boots and Lloyds TSB have signed up to join such renowned value creators as Coca-Cola and General Electric.*

Economic Value Added, or EVA, is the most famous measure. Basically the difference between a company's after-tax operating profit and the cost of capital invested in the business, the concept has been trademarked by Stern Stewart, a US management consultancy that puts such store by it that it had a legal spat with rival consultancy KPMG over the use of the idea.

There are many more acronyms out there, and just about all seem to claim to represent approaches that cut to the heart of shareholder value like no other. There is, for example, WACC, or Weighted Average Cost of Capital, essentially the opportunity cost of the assets a company uses. There is also CFROI, or Cash Flow Return On Investment, which provides a methodology for calculating residual values. And there is TSR, or Total Shareholder Return, dividend payments plus capital appreciation created by increases in the share price.

As all these initials suggest, it is an area more prone than most to complexity and technicalities. Various economists and consultants are forever coming up with their own spin on the basic concept. However, fine as this constant search for understanding obviously is, it also helps to explain why this – like many other compelling management concepts that have come before it – has hitherto not been an unmitigated success. Though companies such as M&S, Glaxo and Reuters tend to top lists of

> *Though companies such as M&S, Glaxo and Reuters tend to top lists of best creators of value and most admired companies, there is a danger of the concept being seen as just another financial measure understood by only a handful of people in head office.*

best creators of value and most admired companies, there is a danger of the concept being seen as just another financial measure understood by only a handful of people in head office. As PA Consulting has pointed out, 'many organisations are too busy working out how to measure shareholder value actually to focus on delivering it'.

Some groups are seeking to deal with the understanding gap by running courses aimed at explaining the fundamentals of the shareholder value concept to line managers. However, others are realising that – no matter how thorough and well-attended such programmes are – they will stand little chance of working because the managers concerned will still find it difficult to see how the measures affect what they are doing, let alone how what they are doing affects the measures.

Too often, companies are trying to go down the shareholder value route when they have no foundation for that value. They lack an innovative product or fresh approach to marketing or distribution that gives them a unique selling proposition.

But it is perhaps only a little too cynical to suggest that there is not much mileage in a consultancy telling a prospective client that it has no real hope of creating decent amounts of shareholder value unless it comes up with some idea or strategy that is going to put it at the forefront of its chosen sector. Far better for proponents of the concept to put a lot of effort into establishing a link between plausible economic theory and practical management. The old PW team behind the book *CFO: Architect of the Corporation's Future* claims that by developing a framework from the work of Alfred Rappaport, a US academic whose introduction to the subject, *Creating Shareholder Value*, is the touchstone for those involved in this field, it has identified seven 'value drivers – macro-level factors, varying between industries, that determine shareholder value'. Most of them centre on operations, covering such aspects as turnover growth and cash profit margins, but there are also WACC, a rate of return measure that also takes account of risk, and the timeframe over which the market expects a company to achieve returns greater than its cost of capital – termed the 'competitive advantage period' by the firm.

According to Mike Maskall, one of the firm's leading partners, understanding the value drivers enables him and his colleagues – on the basis of published information – to calculate the value of a company to within 5 per cent of its stock price. For instance, in November 1997, it valued the glassmaker Pilkington at 141p a share when the actual stock price was 143p. The following morning the shares rose to 157p because the company had announced redundancies; when the market had closed, the PW team put that information into its model and came up with a value of 158p.

But, to advisers like Maskall and Mark Thomas, shareholder value specialist in PA's management group, the real power of the models comes through their ability to move the debate beyond the purely financial to cover the so-called soft management issues. Greater sophistication means that managers can 'understand better and better the real impact of their decisions on shareholder value', says Thomas.

Claiming that anything can be converted into its impact on the share price, Maskall points to the example of the pharmaceuticals company that needed to increase the efficiency of its research and development department because it was taking an average of 12 years to get a drug to market. With R&D costs accounting for 20 per cent of annual sales, a reduction in the time to market of just a year would produce significant savings. However, the company had a morale problem that would make such an improvement difficult. Research discovered that the employees felt an improvement in this area could be achieved if an Intranet were installed to aid communication between different researchers and if management listened to suggestions and ideas from employees. The Intranet was set up and the management was persuaded to change its approach. Morale improved and the market upgraded the stock.

None of this would come as much of a surprise to our hero companies, such as Hewlett-Packard and 3M, of course. It is merely mathematical support for something that they seem to know intuitively.

By saying that it is now taking this modelling into the sphere of helping companies decide which levers or 'beer pumps' to pull when competing with rivals, PwC is really demonstrating the constant desire on the part of consultants to break down the art of succeeding in business into some form of mechanical process. It is tantamount to saying that, if you just do this and this and pay attention to that at the same time, you cannot fail.

But, of course, business is not like that. The real successes, especially in these turbulent times, are not master planners and schemers but those with what appears to be an innate sense of where the market is going and a notion of how to prosper from it. As can be seen from the constant and often-derided attempts by the established financial services players to catch up with the more fleet-footed direct services, too much analysis can get you left behind. That is not to say that companies should be totally lacking in structure and controls, but it is to say that they should not shackle themselves too tightly.

In their efforts to help their clients break free from such constraints, in this age of empowerment consultants have been pointing to the importance of making shareholder value the basis for decision making at all levels of the company.

As Deloitte Consulting's John Donovan, Richard Tully and Brent Wortman point out in their book *The Value Enterprise*, 'only when people understand their role in an organisation and clearly perceive how they can contribute to value, is value creation going to take place on any significant scale'.

Of course, one of the most effective ways of achieving this is to make a link between value creation and pay. PA has found itself particularly associated with the shareholder value concept because its chairman, Jon Moynihan, has been a vociferous proponent of aligning executive remuneration with long-term value creation rather than with the more traditional stock options and other generally short-term incentive schemes that have turned out to be rather generous in recent years.

But the firm – which is so wedded to the idea that all its employees, not just those at the top, have some element of their pay linked to performance – realises that the approach needs to stretch much further. As co-sponsor of the British Quality of Management Awards, a five-year exercise that aimed to raise the standard of management through identifying the key factors behind performance, it has repeatedly criticised companies for routinely destroying shareholder value.

Gavin Barrett, a member of the firm's management group, has pointed to the high failure rate of projects and various attempts to 'relationship manage' customers as particular causes of destruction. In the report on the 1998 awards, he said: 'A great deal of corporate effort goes into managing a form of "leaky bucket". Only when value created exceeds value destroyed is there a net gain for shareholders.'

> 'A great deal of corporate effort goes into managing a form of "leaky bucket". Only when value created exceeds value destroyed is there a net gain for shareholders.' – Gavin Barrett of PA Consulting's Management Development Centre.

However, for those prepared to go to the trouble of pushing the value-based approach throughout their organisations there genuinely seems to be a prize worth winning. A survey by PA found that investing in a company adopting a shareholder value approach would over 10 years produce twice the return of putting money into a company that had not gone down this road.

Moreover, claims Maskall, the sort of measures that would result would be 'much more real' than the somewhat technical figures that have contributed to the problems of the past. 'Previously, it was like driving looking through the rear-view mirror; now, you're looking through the windscreen,' he says.

However, just as a select group of high-class companies feature in the various books setting out particular approaches as the route to the Holy Grail of sustained success, so the Sundridge Park/Mori initiative identified a small group of British companies, headed by Marks & Spencer and including Glaxo Wellcome and British Airways, that appear to be head and shoulders above the rest.

Nevertheless, it is hard to escape the feeling that by going so relentlessly down what might be termed the 'it's the shareholders, stupid' approach, companies are demonstrating that they really are the financially obsessed organisations they are depicted as. They might go on about their community activities, about their balanced scorecards and about their concern for the different stakeholders, but when it really comes down to it, the profit motive is overwhelming.

The potential emptiness of the shareholder value approach can be seen in the spate of demergers of the late 1990s that the concept helped to spawn. Along with the renewed interest in focus, the demand to fix on enhancing returns for investors can be seen as being behind the drive to 'release the value' in companies. Stuck in the figurative backrooms of companies, this stuff was apparently sitting there, just waiting for the right deal miraculously to release it.

The variation on the parts are greater than the sum has seen a host of break-ups – notably AT&T and the 'Baby Bells' in the United States, British Gas, Hanson, the creation of Zeneca out of ICI and the splitting of Thorn and EMI into, respectively, a rentals business and a music group.

However, all has not always worked out as planned. Hanson's break-up released very little value for investors on the grounds, it was said, that the various operations had been so tightly run that there was little value left to emerge. So why was the deal done, other than to satisfy the demand to abandon conglomerates and the sorts of corporate frippery never associated with Hanson?

Similarly, where is the long-term value in splitting a group like Thorn EMI into two groups that have both been seen as takeover targets so often that it must be difficult to do any kind of long-term planning within? Indeed, the Thorn business was put out of its misery in June 1998, when Nomura decided it could do something with the rentals income that had so far eluded its previous management.

WHY INVEST WHEN YOU CAN GIVE THE MONEY BACK TO SHAREHOLDERS?

Nothing better illustrates the fixation with improving returns for shareholders than the widespread enthusiasm for share buybacks. Both 1997 and 1998 saw billions spent by companies on various forms of purchasing their own shares. Sure, the investors were happy – thanks to their enhanced dividends – but think of the signal that is being sent out by such actions.

Put basically, it amounts to: we have all this cash sloshing about in the coffers and we can think of nothing to do with it that will enhance the value of your investments, so you might as well have it back and put it into something more worthwhile. As a spokesman for Reuters, the business information group, said when it became one of many well-known companies on both sides of the Atlantic to announce a buyback in 1997 and 1998: 'If shareholders can make better use of the funds than the company can, then the company should return them.'

Now, the picture is complicated by the various fiscal reasons for taking such action. And some companies are savvy enough about the operation of the markets to realise that just talking about an initiative of this sort can be enough to bolster a flagging share price. But there is no escaping the fact that this is a negative approach to business.

Surely, the business of business is to do business, not to shy away from it on the grounds that it cannot think of the right sort of thing to do. Even if there are no obvious opportunities in a company's own sector, there is nothing to stop it trying its hand – probably on a limited basis – in other areas of activity.

Can it be a coincidence that some of the world's most innovative companies – such as the Virgin group and Cisco Systems – have highly active venture capital programmes?

Carrying out exercises like share buybacks because they are fiscally convenient, breaking up businesses purely to get the 'value' out of them rather than because it might make them more agile and competitive, or embarking on defensive mergers all smack of a safety-first, management-by-the-numbers approach.

Many of the companies that have joined in the enthusiasm for buybacks are the sort that will jump on any management bandwagon. To these sorts of organisations, the important thing is to say the right things – have you noticed how similar are the statements made by senior executives at annual results announcements? – and cotton on to those techniques that will keep things rolling along for just a bit longer – whether it is a financial services group linking up with another, spinning off a 'non-core' part of the business or giving back shareholders a portion of their funds. It is little wonder that the employees of such organisations are lacking in energy and spirit; the last sort of initiative effectively sends a message that we, the management, will boost our perceived performance through a little financial trick rather than by trusting you, the employees, to go out there and develop promising businesses.

The late 1990s have seen the enthusiasm for buybacks become so popular that companies that have many great qualities but are a little unsure of their place in the modern world – such as Reuters, which has done some corporate venturing, and Shell – have fallen into temptation. While it is easy to understand the reluctance to stand out from the crowd, one cannot help but feel that such organisations are selling themselves short by throwing in the towel in this way. Both have extensive histories of reinventing themselves – and both have gone in for ventures outside their central areas of business.

So, why should they shrink from the challenge?

Part of the reason lies in the way that the markets work; once one company has found a way of delighting its shareholders, the pressure is on for others to follow suit. Just as many organisations attributed their over-extensions of the late 1980s to pressure from the markets to keep up their growth. To this day, many commentators seem overly prepared to accept companies' claims that all is fine, even when there are various factors that might suggest otherwise.

However, it is not reasonable to claim, as many organisations seek to do, that they have to resort to this sort of thing because the markets – be they Wall Street, the London Stock Exchange or elsewhere – do not understand such concepts as innovation and organic growth. All the surveys show analysts putting innovation and sustained growth well up their lists of preferred characteristics. But above all, markets value management. And it is a sad fact that effective management is not nearly in such good supply as all those telephone number salaries would suggest.

In fact, there seems to be a requirement for many managers to develop the art of making excuses when conditions are against them. Disadvantageous exchange rates and adverse weather conditions are two reasons favoured by British managers for depressed results.

On the other hand, when the results are good, there is little talk of beneficial exchange rates (unless, of course, they were immediately preceded by the other sort) and of the weather. Then it is all down to the quality of the management, and, possibly, the contribution of employees.

But really what such organisations are admitting is that they are at the mercy of the economic cycle and whatever approaches to business are current at the time. Since employees are generally highly astute at picking up on what drives their organisations, it is hardly surprising that managers do not find the sort of commitment and motivation the books say they should be seeking.

Though the general perception is that much business, if not all, is like this, there are organisations in which the sense of business being a great adventure persists. In some, there is even a feeling that it might be fun as well as hard work.

It is easy enough to understand how the proprietors and staff of the internationally renowned British product design company Seymour Powell might find it highly enjoyable to be at the leading edge of product development and in demand for their assistance with everything from train carriages and motorcycles to cameras and women's lingerie. After all, anybody who has seen the appearances of Richard Seymour and Dick Powell on British television will know how they are constantly excited by the work they do.

Convinced that 'turnover is vanity', Seymour and Powell head a very small organisation. But the same sense of purpose can be had at large organisations, too. Even ones as 'uncool' as steel production and power generation. Just listen to Ken Iverson.

His company, Nucor Steel, is one of those organisations that have created a sense of engagement so that employees – and in the most effective companies, customers, suppliers and the community at large – voluntarily sign up for what it is about, rather than having to be 'brought onside' or coerced.

Iverson is familiar to management writers because Nucor is credited with turning the US steel industry on its head. At a time when the large integrated mills – much like British Steel and other European producers – were locked into a downward spiral of falling prices, cost-cutting and redundancies, this little-known company based in Charlotte, North Carolina was growing by entering new markets and trying out new processes. In his recently published book *Plain Talk*, Iverson writes: 'We're big on informality, caring, freedom, respect, equality and the simple truth. We have little tolerance for the politics, the pettiness, the fixation on rank and status and the insensitivity to employees.'

In Britain, the Virgin empire founded by Richard Branson has a similar lack of stuffiness that does not end with the chairman and chief executive's well-known fondness for woolly jumpers. Branson himself is not to everybody's taste, not least because of his most un-British love of publicity, but there is no denying his commitment to the many and varied businesses that his group now operates.

As he said in his Department of Trade and Industry-sponsored Innovation Lecture in March 1998, it is easy to imagine people having fun in his original enterprise, the record industry. But he and the thousands that now work with him had shown that it was possible to take the same sort of attitudes into such unpromising fields as pensions, life assurance and banking. He and his colleagues stress, of course, that being a business rather than a charity means that making money is a priority, but they are also adamant that this should not prevent the occupation being enjoyable. It is perhaps for this reason, above all others, that Branson has become an inspirational business leader for younger people.

What links the various Virgin enterprises together is a commitment to customer service; and the key to success, he repeatedly told his audience, was getting the right people and giving them the freedom to get on with the job. Certainly, those who have advised the group attest to the quality of the people with whom they have dealt. They may not be strong on standard business attire, but they know what they are doing and they have a clear sense of what they are seeking to achieve. In typical colourful style, they talk of the ideal business opportunity for Virgin being a sector where there is 'a big, bad wolf' – a company that is overcharging and under-delivering.

Significantly, too, the managers running the various businesses – whether it is the transatlantic airline, the cinema chain or the financial services operation – all agree on the importance of themselves and the people working alongside them. Striving not to be immodest, they insist that Branson – although arguably the most visible chief executive since Victor Kiam bought Remington Shavers – is not so influential that the businesses would not survive without him. Their message appears to be that he has merely created an atmosphere in which the creativity of them and their colleagues can flourish.

But, though the importance of people is increasingly being acknowledged by a variety of organisations, business performance is not just about this. Companies that build sustainable success seem to have a certain something about them – what the London Business School's Sumantra Ghoshal calls 'the smell of the place'.

In *The Individualized Corporation,* he and Harvard Business School professor Christopher Bartlett quote a manager met during their researches as saying: 'Walk into any office or factory, and within the first 10 minutes you will sense the smell of the place. You will sense it in the energy and the hum of work, you will see it in the eyes of the people, in how they walk and talk. You will sense it in a thousand small details all around you.'

This can work in negative as well as positive ways. As Ghoshal and Bartlett point out, whether described as culture, climate or context, 'it is the smell of the place that prevents companies from creating the capabilities of entrepreneurship, learning and self-renewal' that they see as so vital to long-term success.

Their favoured victim in the explanation of this theory is Westinghouse, the US industrial company which in recent years has come out second best to its long-term rival General Electric, a media favourite of the 1990s. They claim that the company is a particularly apt choice because over the past decade and a half it has 'declared victory in the battle for change – not

once but three times, each time to stumble and begin the process all over again.'

The story is a graphic one – beginning with Robert Kirby –
after a period of massive restructuring spanning the whole second half of the 1970s – announcing an end to the company's
history of 'unpleasant November and December surprises'.
Ghoshal and Bartlett quote him as referring to the constant
complaint that slack internal controls had given the company
a reputation as accident-prone with the words: 'We have killed
the beast. We are at the beginning of an era of uninterrupted
growth.'

By 1983, just two years later, though, a sharp deterioration
in results led to a fresh round of changes in strategy, structure,
systems and chief executive. And the effort paid off so that by
1987, when the return on equity topped 20 per cent and beat
that of GE, Kirby's successor, Douglas Danforth, announced
that Westinghouse had entered the winner's circle – a select
group of elite corporations that had a reputation for consist-
ently good financial performance and strong management.

But just another year later another setback brought a new
chief executive in the shape of John Marous, who set off another round of changes by declaring a vision of lifting the company from its then status as a good corporation to a great one.
Two years later, with sales growing at more than 10 per cent a
year and net profits running at nearly a billion dollars, success
seemed so certain that *Fortune* magazine took over the job previously handled by the company's management and put the
company on its cover with the legend 'Respect, At Last'.

Almost inevitably, just another two years later, what Ghoshal
and Bartlett term 'a massive mess at Westinghouse Credit –
perhaps the biggest "surprise" in the company's history –
plunged the group into a 1992 loss of $1.7 billion' and led the
stock price to fall to half its level at the time of the *Fortune*
accolade. Then chief executive Paul Lego could not see the storm

and handed over to Michael Jordon, who – of course – announced 'a new beginning'.

Though it is a stark example – made more so by being committed to print like that – it is not really so uncommon. Any regular reader of the business pages of any serious newspaper in the industrialised world will be familiar with the constant lurches in strategy undertaken by successive managements of publicly quoted companies. They will also know how these executives constantly stretch credulity by suggesting that what in the past has largely served a company well is suddenly total nonsense and that what has in the past been discredited is suddenly going to be the answer to all their ills.

In Britain, the story is in many ways similar to that of the car producer now known as Rover Group. Successive chief executives from Sir Michael Edwardes on have been credited with turning the company around only for it to be still losing millions of pounds a year in late 1998 and seen as a vivid illustration of the productivity gulf between Britain and the newly resurgent Germany.

If the sorry tale of Westinghouse – which has over the past two decades seen its revenues remain fairly flat at around the $10 billion mark, while those of GE have soared from a bit more than $15 billion to about $80 billion – and countless other similarly 'lost' companies shows anything, it is that all the techniques in the world, all the brainiest consultants and all the most determined senior executives will count for nothing if no effort is made really to change attitudes and the ways in which things are done.

Ghoshal and Bartlett make their point by contrasting the experience of a single manager under the control, first of Westinghouse and then of ABB, after it takes control of the division in which he works.

Don Jans, at the time the authors met him in the early 1990s, was general manager of a part of ABB's transmission and distribution business that – under Westinghouse – had had a record of limited profitability and little growth. But in the four years since the European company had acquired it, revenues had gone up by 45 per cent and profits by 120 per cent.

Though this transformation of a mature operation into a business with the characteristics of a young high-growth company is remarkable enough, it is made more so by the fact that Jans and his colleagues were kept on by the new management. In contrast to the old view that the only way to get such results is to shake out the personnel on the basis that people become imbued with bad habits that cannot be changed, ABB found a way of getting the best out of what were by any standards talented individuals.

Being academics, Ghoshal and Bartlett suggest that what had been discovered was 'the magic of the Individualized Corporation, built on the bedrock of individual initiative at all levels of the company'. Encouragingly for them, the experience of the long-time Westinghouse men was echoed elsewhere – for instance, at ISS, the Copenhagen-based global cleaning services company.

They also see 'the same spirit of individual initiative' driving employees in a team at 3M, the US-based company that defies current thinking about corporate structure by daring to be a diversified industrial group making products that range from Post-it Notes to medical devices.

But at 3M nobody is likely to think in terms of working for an 'individualised corporation' just as they are unlikely to be overly troubled by the fact that their organisational chart has flummoxed countless management thinkers over the years. This is a company that seems to have almost naturally come up with the best way of managing its people and operations – and that is largely to leave them to themselves. It is one of the clearest examples of the 'smell of the place' working in a positive sense.

Whether you visit their operations in the UK or their main locations in the United States, in St Paul, Minnesota and Austin, Texas – each very different – the 'sense of purpose' that is

much talked and written about, but sadly elusive in most organisations is very much in evidence.

One of the most obvious ways in which this manifests itself
is in the fact that throughout the company – from the company's deputy chairman to a junior employee putting together
electronic components at a factory in Austin – it is apparent
that everybody knows not only their role, but also where this
fits into the plan for the organisation as a whole.

People in such organisations are not all mindless automa-
tons, scared stiff of voicing anything but the party line. Such is
their confidence that openness is genuinely
encouraged rather than paid lip service, and
such is the respect granted employees by the
company that they will openly question, or at
least discuss with outsiders the wisdom of strategic decisions. Also, far from seeking to
present themselves as all-knowing heroes, senior executives will tell you how they took much
longer than colleagues to see the potential of
products that are now highly successful, or else
made decisions that – with the benefit of hindsight – can now be seen to be wrong.

> *Far from seeking to present themselves as all-knowing heroes, senior executives will tell you how they took much longer than colleagues to see the potential of products that are now highly successful, or else made decisions that – with the benefit of hindsight – can now be seen to be wrong.*

This also seems to be the case with HP. Even
a trip to the UK administrative headquarters at Bracknell, Berkshire leaves the visitor with the clear impression that this is a
company with a well-developed awareness of what it is trying
to do. At the company's laboratories in Bristol, where a third
of the computer and electronics maker's worldwide research
and development is carried out, there is even more of an air of
purpose, of confidence.

At both locations, conventional offices are at a minimum.
Even senior executives are seated in open-plan offices broken
only by partitions – though there are private rooms for meetings. And the energy is obvious – not in lots of bustle, which

can really be a lot of mindless chasing about, but in a quiet sense of purpose.

Moreover, just as at 3M, senior managers – though highly trained scientists – are apt to talk about a need for engagement, chiefly between their workforces and their customers. They know that it is no good them just coming up with impressive products or services; they have to be the sorts of things that customers want so badly that their arrival leads to a bond being formed.

Such companies are far from being alone in this. You can feel the same sort of force on visits to many small and medium-sized enterprises, and even at some much larger companies that are still privately owned. But it is true that far too many businesses seem intent on doing just enough to get by. The building contractor who said that his success in picking up business around the world was attributable to three things – doing what he said he would do, turning up on time and cleaning up after himself – spoke volumes for the attitudes of his competitors. Everybody is familiar with businesses – not just in building but in many other sectors, too – where not just the workforce but also the owners appear to have no real commitment.

> *Senior managers – though highly trained scientists – are apt to talk about a need for engagement, chiefly between their workforces and their customers. They know that it is no good them just coming up with impressive products or services; they have to be the sorts of things that customers want so badly that their arrival leads to a bond being formed.*

Often companies that start out with a positive, highly participative approach lose it as they become large corporations. Much of this is probably to do with the bureaucracy that seems to rampage as executives seemingly take the view that they will not be taken seriously by City advisers and other outsiders if they do not give themselves perks and privileges. Not surprisingly, such moves tend to be accompanied by, or lead to, a loss of focus on their products and markets. Accordingly, where previously they would have made it their business to know everything about the conditions in which their businesses operated, they tend to delegate that to others, with the result that it is rare that anybody – and certainly not the top executives – has a complete picture of what is going on. Even though outside expectations will typically force them to give the impression that they do.

At companies like Virgin, 3M and HP, they do not go in for such pretences. For a start, they break up the business into manageable business units (and this is an evolving process, so that units are constantly being monitored to ensure that they are not becoming too unwieldy).

At Virgin, for instance, the staff like to think of the organisation as 'a big, small company' in that, while part of a large group, the units think and act as if they were individual small businesses. Branson talks of resisting the accountants' entreaties to reduce costs by getting the various units to share call centres and other areas of operation that many businesses tend to think of as merely support units. His argument is that if such facilities are made part of a team doing identifiable work, whether taking flight bookings or selling pensions, the people in them are more likely to be enthused about what they are doing – and so do it better. It is the sort of thing that is likely to get them out of bed in the morning, he says.

Such businesses also genuinely devolve responsibility and power to the people running those operations. For example, 3M's deputy chairman, Ron Mitsch, has recounted how a senior manager in one of the company's operations was explaining the need for a sizeable investment to support a new product. Mitsch's response was that it was a waste of time this executive seeking to justify this expenditure to him when he could not possibly know enough about that particular part of the business to make the decision. If the executive thought the money needed to be spent, he ought to get on and do it.

Similarly, Rex Query, controller (effectively second in command) of a steel plant operated by the US steel company Nucor, tells of how when he was given this managerial role after an initial spell at the company's headquarters he was visited by the company chief executive, John Correnti. 'He said, "You will make a lot of bad decisions and will cost this company millions of dollars. Please don't make them all in one year." I have the freedom to mess up. I've never once worried about making a mistake,' says Query, who qualified with a large accountancy firm before making his move into industry.

> *'You will make a lot of bad decisions and will cost this company millions of dollars. Please don't make them all in one year.'*

One of the classic examples of the apparently successful insistence on making even a large company behave with the vigour and enterprise of a start-up is Cisco Systems, the immensely successful Silicon Valley-based supplier of Internet products and services.

As a Brit, Paul Mountford is wary of management clichés. But even he admits that the company, of which he is the UK managing director, is special. 'It's the closest place I've ever worked to a meritocracy', he says, explaining that the style is informal and open-door to the extreme – but very much focused on success.

Though few people outside the computer industry really understand what the company does, it has in the decade or so that it has been in business acquired an enviable reputation for the way in which it is managed. The middle manager at a rival company, who talked of the 'passion' exuding from the employees he met on a tour of one of its facilities, is typical. Mountford describes how he has been asked how the company manages to ensure that everybody working there knows the crucial issues facing the organisation.

The answer seems to lie in a combination of the peculiar hot-house atmosphere of Silicon Valley and the vision of the founder, John Chambers. The former is only a partial explanation, for while technology is leading many organisations in the area to operate according to the philosophy of teamworking and flat hierarchies, not all of these admittedly highly innovative groups are growing at the pace of Cisco. By 1998, the company had annual revenues of $6.8 billion, having expanded a hundredfold since going public in 1991, and had a market capitalisation of about $65 billion – ahead of General Motors and BT. Renowned for hiring about 1000 people a quarter, it employed 11,400 staff in 54 locations around the world.

Mountford attributes a large part of this success to the management style epitomised by Chambers. A 'people person' rather than a technologist, Chambers reputedly hires people in his own mould. But, rather than being mere mouthpieces, they are encouraged to get things done in the ways that they think fit; there are few definite reporting lines, with the result that a comparatively lowly employee has access to the founder if he or she feels that managers are not taking sufficient account of their ideas or responding to a customer need in the right way.

Customers are core to Cisco, says Mountford. Together with employees, they drive the company. 'Ideas come up from customers to the core of the company and go down very quickly', he adds. Moreover, having been at Wang at the time it started to lose its way, Chambers has developed a 'healthy paranoia about listening to customers'.

This is particularly important because Cisco repeatedly claims it has never been able to dominate its part of the technology world in the way that, say, Microsoft or Intel have. As Mountford says: 'A huge amount of companies much bigger than us are now our competitors.' And, though the company has grown to such a size, Chambers still sees it as an important part of his role to keep abreast of developments in the market and send suggestions on how to respond to them via voice mail to his executives around the world.

However, as a people-oriented manager, Chambers has always realised that it is a lot easier to keep customers on side if the employees are happy, too. Accordingly, all employees – whatever their level – receive stock and so there have been many beneficiaries of the company's staggering rise.

The fondness for teamwork is also connected with this phi-losophy on the basis that 'high-performance teams are all about mutual respect'.

However, nobody should be fooled into thinking that all this means that Cisco is an easy place to work with extraordinary success shielding underperforming individuals. The drive against costs is as relentless as any in the more traditional industries struggling to remain afloat. The difference is that resources released in this way are not sent straight to the bottom line, but are diverted to places where they can help increase revenues.

> *The drive against costs is as relentless as any in the more traditional industries strug-gling to remain afloat. The difference is that resources released in this way are not sent straight to the bottom line, but are diverted to places where they can help increase revenues.*

Contrast this with how all those British utili-ties that you are forced to deal with seem so intent on using call centres to keep you – the customer – at bay. When they say, as does Brit-ish Gas on its bills, that you should avoid call-ing at certain times, you instinctively feel they are cutting costs. A company that really cared about customer service would re-spond to the fact that Monday was very busy by opening on Sunday as well as Saturday. Working such hours need not be exploitative; handled properly, such initiatives can, of course, increase employment.

Also, while Cisco clearly has an even greater incentive than most to make use of technology, it seeks to restrict it to those roles where the tools can do more cheaply what humans do without dragging down customer service.

By way of example, he cites how last year the company used the Internet to create a support system that enabled customers to gain direct access to the company and help themselves. The move saved the company about $350 million, or about 20 per cent of its fixed costs. But more importantly, it helped rectify a shortage of engineers that was threatening to hold up the com-pany's 35 per cent a year growth plans. As part of the initia-tive, 1000 engineers have been transferred from customer support to research and development, and therefore help future expansion.

It is in striking contrast to the usual management approach, which takes what is effectively a one-off boost straight to the bottom line. As well as being negative, this is extremely short-sighted, since – rather like the selling-off-the-family-silver asset sales associated with Britain's Conservative governments of the 1980s and early 1990s – it amounts to a squandering of unusual advantages for short-term gain.

Indeed, Mountford points out that this exercise has been doubly effective since, although costs were cut, the company's customer satisfaction rating actually went up.

But, while Cisco can boast steady growth over its short history, rather than the more common 'spikes' signalling erratic expansion, it is conscious that it is caught in a bit of bind through being rather large by the standards of Silicon Valley start-ups. Consequently, it faces extremely tough competition for the best recruits on the grounds that many of them are drawn to the 'hipper' IT companies.

But, for all its size, it is not above a bit of guerrilla warfare. Knowing that staff from competitors often visit the Cisco Website in order to seek information about products and the like, it has set things up so that any visitors first have to pass through the company's recruitment pages. On its own, this move has saved several million dollars in recruitment costs over recent months, but it also helps to create a buzz about the company. Web surfers can match their skills to openings at the company simply by searching by a keyword, or they can even submit their CVs online.

Perhaps more important, as an article in a recent issue of *Fast Company* magazine pointed out, is the ability to pair up with a 'friend' inside the company who will introduce the visitor to the right people and lead them through the hiring process.

By working in a way that also involves advertising the Website at other sites which the sort of people it is seeking are known to frequent, the company is able to tap into people who are happy in their current positions as well as the habitual job hoppers. As an executive quoted in the same article says, 'we actively target the passive job seeker'.

And if this is not enough, the company is using its Internet product expertise to develop wheezes that help make job seekers feel more secure – including screen disguises that can be activated at the touch of a key so that if a superior suddenly walks by the job seeker can appear to be working on something innocuous.

However, for all the technological wizadry, Cisco appears to be determined to prove that being big and techie does not mean that it cannot be people-focused. Indeed, executives insist that it is this focus that is behind its extraordinary success.

Which is why Chambers has a tradition of breakfasting with several dozen rank-and-file employees each month. With everybody encouraged to give voice to their views on the company, the sessions can apparently often be bruising encounters for the founder, but they are seen as a vital means of keeping in touch with grass-roots opinions. 'I learn a lot about what's really going on. The employees ask tough questions, and by the time you've heard something a couple of times, you know you've got a problem – or an opportunity,' he told an interviewer in early 1998.

Chapter 4

PUTTING THE VALUES INTO VISIONS AND MISSION STATEMENTS

If ever business people have succeeded in inviting people to pour scorn upon them it is in their espousal of missions, visions and values.

It is not just that, as with anything written by a committee, the wording of these statements comes out so tortured. Nor is it that, once you have worked out what all the jargon and gobbledegook means, the documents are more statements of the obvious than the inspirational texts they are held out to be. It is the fact that – in as much as these statements ever get into anything visionary, missionary or value-laden – they are at such variance with reality.

With few exceptions, business has little to do with values. In fact, it is still largely the case that business leaders expect their employees to leave whatever values they may have at the door and get on with business.

The problem is not so much that people in business are wilfully dishonest, underhand or whatever. It is just that they tend not to see that values or ethics amount to an issue in business today. Sadly, modern developments in business have made it a much more explicit cause of concern.

Downsizing and its attendant delayering have pushed people into positions of responsibility at a much younger age and with less experience than would previously have been the case. And without the 'grey hairs' to advise them, they can be inclined to let their enthusiasm and eagerness to get the job done colour their judgement. Equally, the constantly expanding size of most organisations means that it is not only impossible to know everybody, but it is difficult to ensure that standards are maintained. This is particularly a problem when organisations are taking on recruits from different countries – what is right in one culture might not be in another.

Though increasing numbers of organisations – particularly banks and other financial services organisations – are installing codes of conduct in an effort to spell out what is expected of staff, very few have well-established sets of principles like those enshrined in the HP Way to help employees stick to the straight and narrow.

Even when they do seek to acknowledge that values have a place in businesses, executives tend to get it wrong. Business people talk a lot about missions, visions and values these days because that is what their marketing advisers tell them the customers want to hear.

This is not to say that the public is not interested in the issue. You only have to look at the success of the Body Shop and the Co-operative Bank since it announced its ethical policy to realise that they are. Moreover, in the run-up to Christmas of 1998, when retailers up and down Britain were bemoaning their fate, the *Financial Times* noted that sales at Traidcraft, which sells products made by small traders in the poorest countries, soared.

However, reputation, integrity and the rest are in acute danger of becoming little more than marketing slogans for the vast majority of companies – simply because the words are trotted out with little thought and scant attempt to establish whether the organisations concerned really measure up to such standards, or have any serious intent to do so.

Yes, in high streets crowded with too many stores that look the same, consumers will seek out the companies with which they feel comfortable doing business. But they are becoming increasingly sophisticated and will not necessarily accept that a company has an ethical stance just because it say it has. People have become much more questioning, with the result that even supposedly values-laden companies can find themselves under suspicion because of practices allegedly carried out by their suppliers.

This difficulty also illustrates the dangers in another modern business phenomenon that has hitherto been accepted as inevitable: outsourcing. On the face of it, it makes great sense – and not just to the specialists in fulfilling these contracts, whether they be the likes of Andersen Consulting and EDS for information technology work, or Rentokil-Initial for cleaning contracts. Get rid of non-core support work and concentrate on your real strengths.

It is all very well – but for the fact that support services are not always as far in the background as senior executives think. Suppliers of such services can play a key role in helping outsiders form opinions of the organisation. Whether or not the lifts are clean and working might make more difference to a would-be customer or partner than the presentation given by a middle-ranking executive. It is one thing for organisations to seek to ensure that such standards are kept up through strict contracts, but it is quite another for it to imbue its supplier with its values and attitudes to business.

If, for example, a utility company seeks to expand its market by supplying, say, gas in addition to electricity, it needs to be careful how it chooses who goes about approaching those would-be new customers. If it appoints a company that is a specialist at conventional, foot-in-the-door cold-calling, this may lead not just to a failure to win the extra business but to a diminished view of the company as a whole.

Some in more traditional industries might sneer at the sorts of things held dear by St Luke's – the zany account rooms, the lack of offices and secretaries and the corresponding use of mobile phones within the building, and perhaps most of all the naming of the agency council the Quest. But behind the desire of Andy Law and David Abraham to put their agency on a different footing to the rest of the advertising industry is a wider-ranging goal.

As recounted in an article describing the then one-year-old firm in the December–January 1997 issue of *Fast Company*, the pair had proposed to their colleagues while still with Chiat Day that they go beyond the elimination of desks and offices to dispose of advertising itself.

'If the engine of 20th century economic growth had been marketing, they argued, the successful companies of the 21st century would prosper through the wilful application of a set of principles first described 2,300 years ago by Aristotle: ethics,' said the article.

> '*The successful companies of the 21st century will prosper through the willful application of a set of principles first described 2,300 years ago by Aristotle.*'

Their view was that in an environment in which communications were split between all sorts of media, 'a corporation's interaction with its stakeholders ultimately would become its most powerful communications medium. Ethics would not be an option; it would be a requirement.'

This is already happening. Forward-thinking companies are giving close consideration to their ethics, not just in the narrow sense of having the right principles of corporate governance and other codes in place, but in the wider sense of having concern for their impact – both good and bad – on the communities that surround them. Consultancies such as SustainAbility and the New Economics Foundation are in heavy demand from companies seeking to conduct social audits on themselves.

OIL COMPANIES REALISE
THEY ARE PART OF SOCIETY

Not so long ago, such affairs were very much a fringe activity – conducted by dedicated mavericks such as the Body Shop in the UK and Ben and Jerry's Ice Cream and the outdoor clothing and equipment company Patagonia in the USA. But times have changed and oil companies, once the scourge of the environmental movement, are in some cases in the vanguard.

Shell, in particular, has drawn on a reputation for being fair and open-minded that has to a certain extent been tarnished by recent events and set out its 'statement of values', while what is now BP-Amoco is making similar efforts, especially through its commitment to solar energy.

Both appear to be motivated by a desire to be at the forefront of thinking in this area rather than constantly having to react to pressure groups. The *Financial Times'* Robert Corzine reports, in a guide to responsible business published by his newspaper in May 1998, on how Shell found itself 'sidetracked by wider social issues'. First, in June 1995, its attempt to dump the obsolete Brent Spar oil storage installation in the depths of the Atlantic Ocean led to a public outcry. Then, a few months later, it was at the centre of international controversy after the then military government of Nigeria executed a minority rights activist called Ken Saro-Wiwa and several of his colleagues who had been critical of the company's involvement in an oil-producing area in the Niger Delta. Critics accused the company, which is the major economic force in the area, of failing to put pressure on the Nigerian government to halt the executions.

As Corzine relates, the two incidents 'put a severe strain on the company's relations with internal and external stakeholders'. And while the share price was not hit, senior managers were apparently 'shocked at how quickly the rules of business had been pushed aside'.

After all, Shell had only embarked on its chosen course of action over Brent Spar after securing all the necessary approvals and consulting the 'traditional' external stakeholders, such as fishing organisations and marine environmental groups. But, adds Corzine, 'it failed to anticipate the unease and outright opposition its actions would trigger in the general public'. Meanwhile, the Nigeria episode demonstrates how easy it is for international companies to find themselves in the midst of scandals that are not of their own making (something perhaps all those organisations keen to make the most of opportunities in emerging markets need to be aware of).

Shell was already embarked upon a corporate restructuring and transformation exercise designed to bring what was perceived to be a rather cumbersome management organisation up to date before these events. However, the problems triggered an internal review of the company's culture and values.

They have led to a recognition by Mark Moody-Stuart, chairman of Shell Transport and Trading, which is the UK arm of the group, that the separation of business from society at large is no longer possible. Explaining that the company had spent a lot of time 'trying to draw a clear distinction around our businesses', he says that it is now realised that such efforts are ineffective in preventing 'incursions' from society.

Critics have argued that Shell had not gone far enough by the end of 1998 in 'cleaning up its act', particularly through remaining in Nigeria. But the company claims that, for instance, by adopting new reporting standards it is in a much better position to ensure that the environmental and social impact of its worldwide activities can be measured and assessed. Moreover, it believes that it can still make a positive contribution in Nigeria.

However, it is perhaps more aware of what might be termed the new reality than others. Certainly, Moody-Stuart seems to recognise that it is as much a myth that analysts do not value environmental commitment as that they do not rate innovation. 'Shareholders want outstanding returns in a way they can feel proud of', he has said.

If anything, Shell's traditional rival, BP-Amoco, is even more aware of the business benefits of an oil company adopting a more progressive environmental stance than others. As the *Financial Times'* Corzine points out in the same publication, the company 'has reaped substantial public relations benefit from a relatively modest position in renewable energy'.

A subsidiary of the company – BP Solar – has captured 10 per cent of the market, and the organisation plans to increase its sales tenfold, to $1 billion a year by the end of the first decade of the 21st century. At the same time, however, it is hopeful of increasing underlying net profits substantially, largely through higher oil and gas output.

The explanation of John Browne, chief executive of what was BP, is that because the oil industry is going to remain the predominant supplier of energy for the foreseeable future, it has to play 'a positive and responsible part' in identifying solutions to the fossil fuel consumption problem.

However, while Browne does not appear keen to project himself as an environmental champion, there is evidence to suggest that the 'business case' basis for BP's commitment to 'progressive' environmental, social and development policies may make the approach last longer than if it was purely born of a desire to improve its image.

As Corzine explains, talk about taking steps to bolster the BP brand or enhance its reputation is backed up by action. For example, the company took the lead in leaving the Climate

Change Coalition, an industry trade group that lobbies against programmes designed to reduce the use of fossil fuels.

Moreover, the company recognises that its prospects – termed by the Centre for Tomorrow's Company its 'licence to operate' – can be enhanced substantially if it is seen to be in line in terms of values with the attitudes and aspirations of the societies in which it carries out its business.

Indeed, realising that social awareness, environmental concern and the rest are all bound up together with improving the chances of long-running success is the key. Just as companies that have concentrated on the financials to the point of ignoring the social aspect have often come unstuck, so too have some that have seen their primary focus as dealing with the environment or social problems.

This has been one of the eternal problems at the Body Shop, of course. Leaving aside the fact that the company has suffered from daring to be different and therefore encouraged more traditionally minded organisations and commentators to find fault, it has not helped itself as a publicly quoted company for giving the appearance of disdain for the City and, by extension, shareholders. It is in all probability a good thing that in early 1998 Anita Roddick stood down from the helm of what is by any standards a ground-breaking company, to allow a professional manager to run it while she pursued her enthusiasms.

After all, a *Fortune* article quoted by John Elkington in his book *Cannibals with Forks* pointed out how, once Roddick and her colleagues had decided to make selling cosmetics something more serious by linking the company's marketing strategy with campaigns by the likes of Amnesty International and Greenpeace, the company's top executives 'began spending an increasing amount of time launching environmental projects rather than revamping the company's ageing product line'.

Similarly, Patagonia, a highly regarded US outdoor clothing and equipment company noted as much for its support for environmental and other good causes as for the quality of its goods, almost collapsed in 1991 largely because of founder Yvon Chouinard's reluctance to treat the company as a proper business. An article in the January 1997 issue of the US magazine *Outside* described how his 'passion was limited to what he thought of as the creative side of the business and to making the workplace – with flex time, day care and other liberal benefits – one of the most humane anywhere.'

He refused to think about how the company would pay for this corporate ideal and whenever he was forced to consider company finances, he reputedly likened it to 'getting do-do on your hands'. Indeed, the article quotes one of several chief financial officers to have left the company as saying: 'It's almost a loathing. But that stuff is part of business. It's like hating your left arm.'

In the event, collapse was staved off through laying off 120 people, or nearly a quarter of the whole staff. Chouinard has said: 'We finally admitted that we were businessmen and decided that if we were going to be in business it would be on our terms.'

Accordingly, he and colleagues set about stemming runaway growth and getting to the point where success could be measured 'not by profits but by how much good we'd done at the end of the year'.

Since the turnaround, the company – which has long given 1 per cent of sales to environmental causes – has been widely recognised – including by President Bill Clinton – as a socially responsible employer. It has also raised its sights in environmental terms – subjecting itself to a rigorous outside audit in much the same way as Chouinard's friends at the Body Shop and putting in place policies that are intended to make the company 'sustainable for a hundred years'.

With Patagonia grossing more than $150 million by the mid-1990s, its founder was able to say that what he describes as 'an experiment to prove that being ecologically responsible works' had reached the point where 'every time we've done the right thing, it's ended up making us more money'.

But the earlier tribulations were evidence that 'leading with your values', as Ben Cohen and Jerry Greenfield of Ben & Jerry's Ice Cream put it, is not enough on its own. Sure, companies like this (Ben & Jerry's also has revenues of more than $100 million) are proving that success is not dependent upon abandoning any sense of good. But, while it even appears to be true that certain values are essential to success, it is impossible to ignore the financials and related aspects, at least for any length of time.

This, of course, is the appeal of the 'triple bottom line' put forward by Elkington. Set out in the book *Cannibals with Forks*, the concept is rather like the more familiar 'balanced scorecard' in seeking to go beyond financial performance to calculate the full impact and contribution of a given company – in terms of its environmental and social performance as well as the financial bottom line.

Elkington points out that a number of forces are coming together to create the pressure for this sort of approach to looking at business performance. On the one hand, there are the changing values of the public and of the media. On the other there are more traditional factors – including increasingly sophisticated risk management, growing fears in the insurance sector and developing shifts in corporate governance and reporting requirements.

Put basically, things have moved beyond the point where businesses became involved in community activities or supported worthy causes to salve their consciences. Sure, some organisations carry out such activities because they see their public relations benefits (though, in fact, such initiatives have become so widespread that they have little real value of this sort), while others recognise that their employees expect them to do such things.

But those in the vanguard are realising – like Shell and BP-Amoco – that such matters cannot be extricated from doing business. This has long been the view of organisations such as Hewlett-Packard, which encourages its employees to be part of the community in its fullest sense and almost incidentally has donated millions to worthy causes over the years.

Indeed, it is getting to the point where taking account of various societal and community issues has become part of management's decision-making process. The fate of 3M's advertising hoardings business is a case in point.

What once seemed a logical diversification, on the grounds that the company had developed the technology that allows huge billboard posters to be printed quickly and to a high standard, turned into an embarrassment once it was realised that a leading use of such billboards – for advertising tobacco – was incompatible with the company's growing medical products division. The business was sold.

RETAILERS FORCED TO EXAMINE METHODS OF FOOD PRODUCTION

Similarly, Britain's supermarkets have belatedly realised that they need to address consumers' growing concerns about food and they ways in which it is produced. A spokeswoman for J. Sainsbury quoted in the *Financial Times* explained the process.

'It started with consumers asking questions about food safety, then very quickly moved on to the environment, and then to socially acceptable trading,' she said. The result was that retailers were forced to take stock of how their products were manufactured and whether it involved exploitation of any kind.

But such instances are – unfortunately – rare. Indeed, many business people would be hard-pressed to see the problem that 3M had identified. In their minds they are able to compartmentalise things so that they do not have to face up to such responsibilities – and doing anything else they would ascribe to weakness. Rather like politicians, they are often unable to see that problems of perception exist. Rather, as would appear to be the case with the directors of Camelot, the National Lottery operator, when they were under fire for the size of their bonuses, they think that if they insist that there is not a problem there is not one.

Indeed there may not be – for now. But, as the gurus never tire of reminding us, the business world is capable of rapid change – and what is straightforward and tenable one moment is not the next. After all, investing in tobacco stocks was in late 1998 still being recommended on the basis of the strong cash flows such businesses were generating. By the end of the year, however, certain fund managers were beginning to see the danger signs (which, admittedly, would have been obvious far sooner to people with a bit more commonsense than the average City investor) in the legal settlements being made on behalf of smokers who had contracted cancer and other diseases, and ceasing to recommend such investments.

Of course, somebody with an ethical stance would not have seen the short-term expedient in such a policy, but the constant drive for higher earnings encourages such a values-lacking approach.

Companies such as HP and 3M in the USA and the John Lewis Partnership and Marks & Spencer in Britain have generally been able to resist such pressures because they have strong traditions and long periods of success with which to back up their convictions. For other companies it is harder – they seem to take the view that they more or less have to accept that this is what being a serious business entails.

But that is where those leading them have such an important role to play. Those working in such organisations intuitively know that these things are important. In their social lives they do all sorts of things to support them. As a result, they often feel compromised – either explicitly or implicitly – when at work. Ethics and values is one area where the otherwise fertile debate between bottom-up and top-down has no place. It is for company executives to lay down the principles or rules by which the organisation conducts itself. In failing to do this in so many cases they are failing their organisations and indeed us all.

BUDGETS AND WAITING LISTS

However, important as this aspect is, values is not just about ethics. It is also about knowing who or what you are; and, though the problems of Britain's once-lauded National Health Service and British Broadcasting Corporation are all together too complex to fit neatly into one category, it is arguable that they have a lot to do with values. In other words, both organisations are conscious that they have to adapt to modern times, but in so doing have lost sight of what it is that they are trying to be. To put it bluntly, they have lost touch with their roots.

Since we are all familiar with these organisations, we see such failings all the time. They are probably most apparent in the attention apparently given to management structures over getting sick people treated or programmes made. But imagine what it must be like for people who have worked in such organisations for some time. How are they supposed to know what their priorities are?

A research pamphlet, published in June 1998 by the highly respected Institute of Chartered Accountants of Scotland, provides a succinct summary of much that has gone wrong with Britain's National Health Service since the 1980s. Nobody would suggest that the system was perfect before; the 1983 review of the preceding consensus management system by Sir Roy Griffiths had highlighted such problems as institutionalised stagnation, or resistance to change; excessive delays in management's decision making; avoidance of the resolution of contentious issues and the domination of management by the medical profession. But it does not say much for the reforms eventually decided upon and introduced in April 1991 when even accountants are not too impressed by the enhanced role for members of their profession.

The study, 'Inside Hospital Trusts: Management Styles, Accounting Constraints' by Irvine Lapsley, Sue Llewellyn and Gavin Burnett, raised 'serious questions about the efficacy of the internal market', under which self-governing hospital trusts were established as providers of medical care and health boards and GP fundholders became purchasers. Essentially, the authors felt that there were flaws in the operation of the market that threatened its efficiency.

The three hospital trusts the authors studied closely were sited in health boards where there was little competition. The board was a virtual monopoly purchaser of services from local monopolies, 'which undermines the concept of the split between purchaser and provider in the market'.

In addition, there were important accountability issues raised by the split between the purchasers and providers. In particular, suggested the researchers, it appeared that the arrangements by which purchases of health care were decided were flawed on a number of counts, notably that 'the focus of contract negotiation is predominantly on costs and funding, with a lack of consideration of the quality of care.'

In other words, the NHS had – like many other parts of the public sector bent on becoming more commercial – become so focused on the financial aspects that it had seemingly forgotten what its purpose was. It is a failing that is made all the more stark by the fact that, just as government organisations were becoming more commercial in outlook, many private-sector businesses were starting to realise that financial soundness is very often the result of good practice in such areas as customer service and employee motivation rather than the main objective.

Pointing out that a major effect of these flaws was that the contract negotiation process became a conflict-ridden exchange rather than a more considered evaluation of strategies for health care, the academics said: 'There is a consequent emphasis on the short term which destabilises planning within hospital trusts, which have considerable investment and fixed costs.'

In addition, the arrangements set up showed weaknesses in 'accountability relationships' in the split between providers and purchasers, while 'the drive for cash releasing efficiency savings has placed accounting at the centre of the drive for cost savings in hospital trusts'.

These cash-releasing efficiency savings had been given to individual hospitals as part of the process of negotiating for contracts with purchasers, typically local health boards. They operated through hospital trusts being given nominal amounts for services purchased which were then deflated by fixed percentages as an 'efficiency gain'. The immediate effect of such targets was the virtual or total elimination of any increase allowed for inflation – a consequence which, if combined with increased activity caused by, for example, a government drive on waiting lists, had only heightened awareness and significance of accounting information. Much as in the BBC, it had added to the general impression that the system was there to serve the management rather than vice versa.

It is little wonder that for much of the 1990s senior medical staff and NHS managers have been at loggerheads. Though the government of the day might have expected doctors to fight their corner, the criticism of the reforms remained intense right into the late 1990s.

In May 1996, for instance, it was reported that senior consultants were claiming that patients' lives were at risk from the organisation's accounting system. According to an article in *The Times*, the consultants were suggesting that the situation was so serious that care was 'nearing meltdown'. It continued: 'Flagship hospital trusts are reportedly seeing their once efficient departments slowly destroyed by government requirements for trusts to make year-on-year efficiency savings of 3 per cent. But they are not allowed to use any surpluses to increase capital resources, such as beds, in the following financial year. Instead, they have to use them to cut prices.'

Another consequence – particularly serious when it happens in the medical arena – is the lack of communication between different groups. When the market is divided between purchasers and providers and then within that into various 'cost (or profit) centres', it can be difficult to serve people adequately at the same time as meeting business objectives.

A case in point is the situation revealed in late 1997 when a British hospital had to recall more than 90,000 women for cervical smear tests. The episode, labelled Britain's biggest smear test scare, happened at the Kent and Canterbury Hospitals NHS Trust, which was found by an independent inquiry to be characterised by poor and confused management, understaffing, poor training and a breakdown in working relationships.

The report added that there also appeared to be a remoteness and lack of interest in the cytology screening programmes by its consultants as well as an absence of clear line of accountability. Repeated warnings about problems apparently went unnoticed for years.

> *'I have been forcibly struck ... by the different ways in which the introduction of the internal market ... exacerbated an already weak situation.' – chairman of inquiry into smear test scare.*

Of the 91,000 women recalled in February 1996, 1800 had been given the all-clear when in fact they showed signs of problems and 333 were found to be in need of urgent treatment.

Sir William Wells, chairman of the South Thames NHS Region, who headed the inquiry, said: 'I have been forcibly struck ... by the different ways in which the introduction of the internal market ... exacerbated an already weak situation.'

Nor were the Labour government's plans to end the internal markets all good news. As Paul Gosling reported in the *Independent* in early 1998, 'one of the real successes of GP fundholders has been the way they have cut their drugs bills'. An Audit Commission study found that fundholders typically saved nearly 10 per cent of prescribing expenditure compared with non-fundholders – through switching from expensive branded drugs to cheaper generic medicines, not prescribing drugs of limited clinical value and being more reluctant to prescribe antibiotics.

Though the proposed changes received a generally warm welcome, medical staff face having to get used to a new system that could find it hard to produce the sort of benefits they have seen in recent years. Pointing out that the financial incentives – which involved GPs being allowed to retain in their practices some of the savings achieved – were the most important factor in reducing drug bills, commentators stress that this will be the key to the success – or otherwise – of the latest initiative.

Under a system that effectively seeks – in Gosling's words – to 'bring the stricter financial controls operated by fundholders to all GPs' there will be a problem in that 'GPs will have budgets that they may have difficulty in living with.' A lot is going to depend upon how the budgets are set and what doctors do to try to meet them.

It is all very well making the medical profession accountable – and, in particular, giving doctors some idea of the effect of their decisions. But such an approach can be carried too far. You do not have to be a card-carrying member of the Royal College of Surgeons to take the view that an organisation that seemingly puts more effort into hiring managers than into recruiting nursing staff has its values all mixed up.

Nor is there much sign of the shake-up having had any dramatic effect – in the areas that really matter. That is, standards of patient care and the lengths of waiting lists.

SUITS AT THE BEEB

Similar claims about 'the suits' taking over the asylum have plagued the British Broadcasting Corporation in recent years. The problems associated with what appears to be the widespread adoption of management dogma at the BBC are widely known in Britain for two reasons. First, as a result of the television licence fee, everybody feels they have a stake in the corporation. Second, the employees who are disgruntled by the application of the theories are not only rather more articulate than the average; they have access to plenty of media outlets prepared to air their views – for both altruistic and commercial reasons.

Many will dismiss certain of the criticisms levelled at the senior BBC managers since John Birt and his team set about putting into place their changes as the all-too-predictable whingeing of journalists and associated trades aware that they have come to the end of a wonderful thing. And to an extent that is a well-founded scepticism.

As has been remarked before, journalists are perhaps more openly critical of their bosses than any other group of employees. It is a rare employee that does not think that he or she could do a better job than those above him, and journalists have raised this hyper-critical outlook to new levels.

Nevertheless, some of this scepticism appears well-placed, for, while newspapers and other media organisations are constantly eager to criticise others for their management failings, such groups over the years have shown themselves seriously prone to adopting the latest thinking of the management gurus and to genuinely quixotic decision-making.

The BBC is a special case, however. Sure, the place had been suffering from a lack of management before Birt and his co-horts moved in; and some of the changes are hard to fault. Few outsiders, for example, would question the idea of the same reporter compiling material for both radio and television news programmes.

In many other ways, though, the executives at the BBC have been like those corporate boards who have put all their energies into re-engineering or quality programmes and not realised what has been happening outside their windows. They may have made themselves better at doing what they were doing, but while they were improving it has become the wrong thing to be good at.

Consequently, there have been criticisms along the lines of those reported by the *Independent's* Paul McCann in April 1998. 'In ever-increasing efforts to squeeze efficiencies out of its staff, there has been a kind of merger mania going on within its news-gathering operation', he wrote. Pointing out that this had culminated in the building of a three-storey complex at Television Centre that is loaded with state-of-the-art equipment and claims to be the world's biggest newsroom, he added that the problem was that the hundreds of reporters in London and the 200 BBC bureaux around the world served a 'bewildering array of masters' who all wanted separate bills.

The difficulties result not just from the enthusiasm for cost centres and budgets that have belatedly gripped the media world, but the BBC's particular situation, where merging television and radio news and then having reporters supply stories to domestic radio and television news and also the World Service, the News 24 continual news service and the worldwide commercial network BBC World, means that 'managers have made the average BBC correspondent responsible to almost 60 editors'. If regional newsrooms are included, this number rises to more than 100. This sort of pressure has led to complaints of the sort made by the former foreign correspondent Martin Bell, who claimed that reporters have to spend more time talking to camera than talking to sources or otherwise finding and preparing stories.

At the same time, there are accounting pressures brought on by, on the one hand, the merger of the World Service's news with the domestic service and the resulting desire on the part of the Foreign Office to ensure that its grant does not get mixed up with the licence-fee money, and on the other, the pressure from commercial broadcasters claiming that the licence fee is unfairly subsidising the corporation's commercial operations. This latter position means that the organisation has to be able to supply Parliament with transparent accounts showing what the commercial arm pays for news. The result is a lot of complicated paperwork that makes what is supposedly a lean and mean news machine look a lot like an old-fashioned bureaucracy.

However, for all the whinges from disgruntled journalists, the real failings of the BBC lie elsewhere. In particular, successive managements have shown limited vision, remaining stuck in a rather cosy approach to broadcasting and allowing themselves to be broadsided by developments elsewhere.

This is not to say that the BBC has been outdone by its traditional rival ITV; it has proved itself fairly adept at competing at the mass entertainment level, while retaining something of a commitment to the high production values for which it is renowned around the world. Rather, like a company believing that its competitors come only from its own sector of business, the BBC has focused on terrestrial television and been found wanting when beating off the challenge from both satellite and overseas operators.

True, the corporation has now – apparently at the expense of stretching its team of correspondents – launched a day-long news service. But that was pioneered long ago by CNN, a company that when it started out had none of the advantages of the BBC in terms of readymade international bureaux and teams of specialist correspondents. Now, you can argue that CNN was lucky that the Gulf War came along and effectively made it. But that is often the way with business. A good idea is often legitimised by 'lucky' developments.

But just think what the BBC might look like now if, instead of concentrating on all the management changes that have bedevilled the corporation over recent years, its senior executives had – in management parlance – 'leveraged' the World Service into an international network of the sort that has served CNN in such good stead.

That missed opportunity is, however, just one example of how inwardly focused the BBC has become. It is also like underperforming companies in paying more attention to its own woes than to the concerns of its customers, in this case viewers and listeners. It could every now and again – and especially when it is complaining about the level of the licence fee – consider what the viewer of BBC gets for his or her money compared with what they used to. And, yes, the 'Perfect Day' promotional video was a classy commercial from an organisation that supposedly does not believe in such things. But it still begs the question about the Beeb's true commitment to its roots.

The thousands of Radio 4 listeners who have had their schedules shaken up in recent years would provide a clear answer to that. But, elsewhere, too, the corporation has failed to live up to its values. With so much alternative television available elsewhere, many would question whether the BBC needs to be so fixed upon ratings that it is locked with the independent television channels in a relentless downward spiral.

Sport provides a particularly vivid illustration of the gulf between the present and the past. Once the BBC's Grandstand and its various adjuncts, such as Match of the Day, produced what was pretty much heaven for armchair sports fans. By the late 1990s, though, they struggled by on a diet of horse racing, obscure motor sports and the occasional big-occasion spectacular.

Of course, Rupert Murdoch's UK satellite operation, Sky, has been aggressive in buying up the rights to various sports, particularly football and cricket, but latterly rugby and golf, too, on the perfectly sound assumption that once it acquires a critical mass of sports, it will be difficult for any red-blooded male to do without its service.

However, given that Sky is prepared to go to such lengths to secure these rights, it seems a little odd that the BBC has apparently been so ready effectively to curl up and die. It is small wonder that David Elstein, a former Sky executive currently heading Channel 5, described the corporation as 'mesmerised by impossible and inappropriate ambitions' and 'mired in its peculiar history and method of funding'.

> *"The corporation is mesmerised by impossible and inappropriate ambitions and mired in its peculiar history and method of funding.'*

Talk about managing decline. If it goes on like this for much longer, it is not inconceivable that people will refuse to pay the licence fee – and when the detector van arrives in their neighbourhood argue with some conviction that they felt they were immune from prosecution because they never watch the Beeb.

Chapter 5

THE POWER OF INTEGRITY

It is fashionable to lay all the blame for the shortcomings of British management at the door of traditional big business. But the same sort of short-termism and other failings can be seen in many other areas of commerce. Professional service firms, advertising agencies and publishing groups – all sectors that are thought to attract the 'best and brightest' in numbers that the established big players can only dream of – have over the years shown themselves to be just as much in thrall to cost-cutting and generally limited visions as the others.

In advertising and public relations, the spate of takeovers and mergers in recent years is indicative of the general view that many of the people who run these organisations are less interested in building businesses than in building cashpiles in the bank. One minute they are extolling the virtues of their independent existence, the next they are announcing their delight at linking up with MegaPR. Likewise, such trends as the large-scale abandonment of serious newsgathering and the chase of book publishers after a few big blockbusters seems to suggest an acknowledgement that Rupert Murdoch has the blueprint for running that particular industry, while David Maister, the former Harvard Business School academic who has become the leading guru on professional service firm management, believes too many law, accounting and consulting firms have abandoned professional principles in pursuit of quick gains.

The boom times of the mid to late-1990s have brought great rewards to some of the largest firms and kept a few overstretched accountancy and law firms in business, but any downturn is bound to reveal plenty of evidence in support of his view. Meanwhile, the consolidation at the top end of the professions suggests that accountants and consultants, in particular, are following the lead of their clients in believing that being a global player is all about size. It is difficult to escape the notion that much of this activity is driven more by the desire to put the slogan 'world's largest professional services firm' at the top of the notepaper rather than any intention to give clients a better service. And, as for maintaining their partnership status while creating these huge organisations, that looks a lot like trying to have your cake and eat it, too. The man who said a firm ceases to be a partnership when all the partners can no longer fit around the table in a reasonably sized room probably in most cases had it about right.

> *'I have always asserted that while others may seek* jobs, *the defining characteristic of professionals is that they seek* careers.' – David Maister, *expert on professional firms.*

Maister senses a change in recent years. Pointing out that 'in trying to explain what makes professional life different from other (e.g. corporate) walks of life, I have always asserted that while others may seek *jobs*, the defining characteristic of professionals is that they seek *careers*', he says that he has heard many times the phrase 'It's a job – what more can you expect?', and he adds that many 'good and smart professionals' have told him that they do not *expect* to find passion in their work lives. 'Their fulfilment comes from their families, their hobbies and/or their home lives', he writes.

What else, though, can you expect in organisations that demand ever-increasing commitment in terms of hours worked but not apparently of the heart and soul. Sure, such people make good money – though not as much or as quickly as City traders – but they seem to lose the desire to make long-term careers of this work, unless they have inspirational colleagues and clients whom they admire and want to serve well. In too many service firms, client service means giving up control of your life and effectively being bossed about just as much as in any corporation.

While one senior figure in the advertising world still talks of his work as 'the most fun you can have with your clothes on', it is very probable that the life Maister describes – of professionals working their way up through 'keeping their heads down, putting in vast numbers of billable hours on work generated by others, abdicating control over their own work lives to "the machine", and never being required to demonstrate individual initiative' – rings true for many people in that supposedly endlessly exciting world, too.

WHAT AN AUDIT ISN'T

Though individual professionals set great store by and are justly proud of the qualifications they work so hard to attain, professional service firms have an alarming tendency to threaten those principles – in any number of ways, but most notably by trying to become too rich too soon, by getting so close to clients that they find it difficult to offer independent advice and by becoming too big.

In the late 1980s and early 1990s, accountancy firms, in particular, found themselves in the public eye for all the wrong reasons. Britain saw spectacular collapses from companies – such as Polly Peck and British & Commonwealth – that supposedly epitomised the country's revitalised economy, while in the USA there were the savings and loans debacles – and in just about every case there was a large accountancy firm having to explain why its audit – sometimes carried out only shortly before everything went wrong – failed to detect serious problems.

There have been lengthy investigations by government and professional bodies, legal suits and disciplinary hearings, as well as a lot of explanations of 'what an audit isn't' – chiefly, it seems, it isn't a process for detecting fraud – and of how determined fraudsters can defeat even the most zealous auditor.

Accountants were not always hapless saps in these instances, however. It is arguable that because certain of their number went along with, if not actually encouraged companies to develop the financial engineering techniques that accompanied the flurry of mergers and acquisitions seen in the British and American economies in the 1980s, they actually helped create the conditions under which companies would fail.

The area of financial standards was felt to have got so bad in Britain that in 1990 a new regime was introduced with the highly robust David (now Sir David) Tweedie at the head of an organisation dedicated to producing rules that made sense to ordinary investors and were less open to abuse by clever accountants and company directors.

Along the way, many of the big firms made it clear that they felt that all the regulation and attention surrounding audit meant it was an area of business in which they would really rather not be involved. Sure, it was a way of getting 'your foot in the door' with a client, but it was no longer as central to many firms as might have been expected. Far more exciting – and lucrative – were management consulting and legal services.

Of course, nobody has gone further down that road than Arthur Andersen. As late as 1997, most people would have agreed that the Chicago-based operation had, in becoming what appeared to be a genuine integrated global professional services firm grossing annual revenues of $10 billion, confounded the critics.

Not everybody would have wanted to work there – somehow, the firm has never managed to shake off its image as an army of dark-suited and white-shirted clones – but they could not help but admire the rigour Andersen brought to everything it did. While it did not escape entirely the problems of suddenly collapsing clients – most notoriously, the De Lorean car venture designed to inject much-needed industry into Northern Ireland – it was reckoned to have such high standards that only the highest-calibre and most dedicated people made partner and thus became eligible for the reward of substantial wealth at a comparatively early retirement age.

Having set up a separate consulting unit in 1989, Andersen Consulting, specialising in carrying out substantial information technology projects, the firm looked set for success in the much-coveted legal market. In Europe and elsewhere, it had formed alliances with indigenous law firms and appeared to be on the brink of breaking into the higher echelons of the UK legal market. An association with the purposely established Garrett & Co, later simply Garretts, had been the start, and this had been augmented by the acquisition of the respected Scottish firm Dundas & Wilson. But Andersen wanted a top player.

It originally courted Simmons & Simmons, one of many middle-ranking firms seen as being vulnerable to the pincer attack being mounted by the larger regional firms and the increasingly aggressive London offices of US practices. But the talks broke down and Andersen's attention shifted to Wilde Sapte, a reputable City firm that was coming to the realisation that it lacked the resources to achieve its strategy of global expansion without a partner – and professional firms' pockets do not get much deeper than those at Andersen.

Eventually, in mid-1998, that deal was called off, despite having been announced with some fanfare a few months previously. The ostensible reason was that some of the key staff that Andersen wanted were walking out before the deal could be completed. But pointing out that some departures had been announced even before the talks were announced, some observers suggest that the discussions had demonstrated to Andersen that City law firms were possibly not as close to a large accounting operation as Andersen might have thought.

Certainly, accounting firms have moved a long way ahead of their legal counterparts in the way they are run. For some time, the large firms have to varying degrees introduced systems whereby the partners – largely because they number in the thousands rather than the low hundreds at even the largest law firms – devolve management to executive committees. Even such major strategic initiatives as mergers have been explored by these 'boards' long before the partners as a whole are involved in the process.

By contrast, partners in most law firms still expect to have a substantial say in the way that the place is run. Day-to-day management may be entrusted to a handful of people who may or may not give up client work, but the partners as a whole tend to stay involved in the development of strategic issues.

In organisations attempting to set themselves apart from the mass, that is as it should be. After all, all sorts of companies are realising that the way to get buy-in – or, to put it more attractively, engagement – is to make people feel involved in decision-making and the processes leading up to that, rather than expect them just blindly to follow orders.

This can, of course, be cumbersome and can create a situation where the firm appears to be lacking focus, but it is perhaps indicative that – unlike their accounting brethren – lawyers are less likely to see their way of making a living as just another business. They are inclined to take some convincing to put some strategic plan – however well thought-out – ahead of what they think is best for their clients or their practice area.

Another key factor that may be behind the problems experienced by even such a tightly run ship as Andersen in achieving a critical mass in legal services is doubts over the concept of the 'one-stop shop'. The arguments for the notion that customers or clients should obtain everything of a certain type from one place are most forcefully proposed by those considering mergers in the financial services arena; they were, for example, at the forefront of Travelers Group's merger with Citibank. But, as Professor Hamel and his colleagues at his consultancy Strategos have repeatedly pointed out, cross-selling is one of the great myths of business.

It is difficult to argue – as senior partners of both accounting and law firms often do – that their clients are growing increasingly sophisticated and canny, and more inclined to give them only parts of their business (and then only after submitting them to beauty parades), and then to suggest that – given the opportunity – they are just as inclined to make things easier for themselves by obtaining every professional service they need from a single operator. Even a firm as rigorous in pushing standard operating methods throughout its activities as Andersen cannot guarantee that all its increasingly large numbers of far-flung people reach the same high standards or that it is top-notch in everything it does.

> *Even a firm as rigorous in pushing standard operating methods throughout its activities as Andersen cannot guarantee that all its increasingly large numbers of far-flung people reach the same high standards or that it is top-notch in everything it does.*

As Maister says, it is possible that having a varied portfolio might help a firm to grow. But once it reaches a certain size, it seems inevitable that it breaks up into specialist units. After all, is it not a touch ironic that many corporates are seeking to emulate partnerships by breaking themselves up into smaller chunks in which significant proportions of the staff have stakes.

Perhaps the best evidence for this is the acrimonious dispute that broke out between Arthur Andersen and Andersen Consulting at the end of 1997. It had clearly been simmering for some time, with Consulting partners making comments about how they were subsidising their accounting colleagues. But it came to a head at Christmas of that year, when Consulting declared it was seeking arbitration of its claim that Arthur Andersen and the worldwide organisation charged with managing relationships between the two units had broken agreements signed at the time of the division into two separate units eight years previously, chiefly by allowing the accounting arm to stray into the field of management consultancy.

The accountants claimed that the consulting arm was not interested in the sort of projects they were undertaking, preferring instead to tackle huge programmes – usually of a technological nature – for the world's biggest companies. Moreover, they claimed that the alleged rule breaches were only technical in that the limits on deal sizes had been rendered obsolete by inflation. In return, the consulting arm suggested that the accountants were seeking to move away from the increasingly commoditised audit and related services to more lucrative management consultancy – and legal services – work.

In such circumstances, common sense would have dictated protecting what the two firms had built by reframing the split in operations. But the more that Consulting insisted it was a matter of principle, the more apparent it became that the real motivator was money. At the time of writing, it seemed that relations had become so strained that the only course was for the two operations that set the pace for their respective industries to go their separate ways, even with all the problems and confusions that would ensue.

In just a few months the Andersen organisation has seen itself transformed from the firm that everybody else sets its standards by to just another firm. Its domination was a clear factor in the decisions by, first, Coopers & Lybrand and Price Waterhouse and then KPMG and Ernst & Young to merge. It is no coincidence that each deal made great play of assuming the mantle of 'the world's largest professional services firm' that had hitherto graced all of Andersen's communications.

Equally, the fact that even it was apparently finding size difficult to keep a grip on must have played a part in the abandonment of the proposed KPMG–E&Y link-up.

Some of what has happened to Andersen can be put down to the fact that increasingly testing business conditions are forcing rivals to raise their game, so that even pre-eminent firms such as Andersen cannot afford to be complacent. This is not to say that the newly created and reassuringly not-too-imaginatively named PricewaterhouseCoopers will prove more successful than Andersen. The latter still has the benefit of a strong culture reinforced by what has – despite the attempts to buy law firms – been largely organic growth, while the new firm faces substantial management issues, not least those stemming from its commitment to hire thousands of people around the globe.

It also seems that the firm has been more than a little guilty of the sort of complacency of which its consultants would urge their clients to rid themselves. The firm seemed so sharp that even hardened commentators pronounced themselves impressed – and this may have affected the management to the point where they thought they could do no wrong. Certainly, there had long been signs of this – in the arrogance and disdain with which some Andersen people treated rivals.

Indeed, it is only half jokingly said that the firm had no real competitors. What was meant by that was that Andersen was in so many areas that nobody else could equal its breadth. But it is clear that – to some at least – there was more to it than that.

HIGH RISKS

Even firms that resolve to remain within their own sphere of expertise can get it wrong. In 1997 Britain saw what appears to be a stark case of a well-respected law practice risking its reputation by seemingly getting too close to a client whom many in the City already regarded as not quite 'one of us'.

The irony was that the firm in question, Travers Smith Braithwaite, was not in the position of having to fight for scraps from the rich man's table. While not in the top league, the firm had acquired a base of blue-chip clients with quality lawyers to match and was reckoned to be financially sound.

Yet, with the benefit of hindsight, the warning signs were there. Just months before the firm found itself mired in the debacle of the highly contentious – and ultimately unsuccessful – bid by Andrew Regan's Lanica Trust for the Co-operative Wholesale Society, it had been subjected to a not-altogether flattering examination by the lawyers' magazine *Legal Business*.

Pointing out that the firm had not fulfilled the potential spotted a few years previously, it characterised it as having its 'head in the sand' while the legal market had moved on. With the number of big clients dwindling and good lawyers regularly leaving, Travers Smith was effectively going nowhere.

Moreover, there appeared to be little impetus to change. Those most impervious to new ways of doing things were said to be senior partner Alan Keat, head of corporate Christopher Bell and head of corporate finance Nigel Campion-Smith. According to *Legal Business* these three were 'big billers, real City names with formidable reputations and very close to the best clients'. Dominating the firm, they were 'both the firm's greatest strength and its Achilles heel'.

Interestingly, the article concluded by dwelling on the firm's past reputation. Having quoted a former employee as questioning whether a good reputation was as important in the modern market as foresight and market skills, it calls on the firm to wake up to the fact that a strong reputation and good profits now are no guarantee of future success.

Then just a few months later the magazine was reporting on how Keat was writing an apology – 'we accept that our conduct did not accord with the standards which we set ourselves' – to CWS chief executive Graham Melmoth over activities that included Campion-Smith, legal adviser to Regan, having in his files copies of sensitive and highly confidential documents.

The magazine is not noted for pulling its punches with regard to the practitioners in the field it covers. So, although it points out that many in the City felt that Travers Smith had merely been unfortunate and that there was a certain 'there but for the grace of God go I' air to other lawyers' comments, it states quite categorically: 'The Co-op scandal had nothing to do with bad luck and everything to do with bad judgement.' Though there is no evidence that any wrongdoing was knowingly committed by Travers Smith. The article's author, Sarah Marks, points to a series of mistakes that amount to bad management.

Such matters as being too hungry and getting too close to the client are essentially failings of management, especially when they relate to the sort of organisation for which reputation is all-important. Jack Welch, the much-admired head of General Electric of the USA, has been quoted as saying that 'in the end all you have is integrity'. If that is true for an industrial behemoth like his, imagine how much more so it must be for a professional services firm.

It would be unfair – not to say inaccurate – to suggest that Travers Smith Braithwaite is the first firm to have erred in this way. But perhaps the episode, which also tarnished the name of other City advisers, demonstrated that those who thought that the corporate collapses of the late 1980s and 1990s and the attendant fall-out had produced a fundamental change of attitude were being overly optimistic.

In particular, Travers Smith Braithwaite seems to have fallen foul of what many in the City call the golden rule of 'know your client'. Some firms make a point of not working for anybody not considered to be impeccable on the grounds that it is not just a question of risk, it is also a matter of protecting reputations that can be lost much more easily than gained. Moreover, firms are increasingly aware that certain business people actively seek big-name advisers as a means of persuading other firms to set aside any qualms they might have and sign up.

In this case, it was not apparently a question of the firm getting involved in something that was too big or complex for it – which was the case with some of the accounting firms that found themselves in difficult spots in the late 1980s and early 1990s. Campion-Smith, who later resigned because he felt responsible for the embarrassment caused to the firm by the episode, was a formidable lawyer rated highly by rivals and clients alike. Moreover, he had worked for Andrew Regan, the entrepreneur behind the Co-op bid, and his adviser David Lyons before, advising on the deal that led to the creation of Lanica Trust.

However, he did have a method of working that could contribute to problems of this sort. He preferred to run deals on his own without any involvement from his fellow partners.

Such an approach might make some firms worry that they might be unable to do sufficient due diligence on their client. Moreover, there is also the danger of being too aggressive in accepting new instructions. 'One must never be afraid to say no', said a partner at another firm at the time.

It is an approach that the partners of what was Coopers & Lybrand might well have wished they had taken with regard to the late Robert Maxwell, whose business empire collapsed revealing huge debts and a £400 million black hole in its pension funds soon after his death in 1991.

In February 1999, the accountancy profession's top disciplinary tribunal ordered the firm, which is now part of PricewaterhouseCoopers, and four of its partners to pay fines and costs totally nearly £3.5 million after finding that it lost the plot in dealing with the tycoon and certain of the companies in his empire.

The Joint Disciplinary Scheme report stressed that it had not been alleged that the firm caused direct financial loss or caused or facilitated the collapse of the Maxwell empire by its omissions. Nevertheless, it found shortcomings in both vigilance and diligence and a failure to achieve an appropriate degree of objectivity and scepticism, which might have led to an earlier recognition and exposure of the reality of what was occurring. But, though the people involved – like those at Travers Smith – did nothing illegal, it is hard to deny that because of the scale of this scandal great damage has been done to the reputation of one of the accounting professions best-known names.

As Dale Fishburn, co-founder of Fishburn Hedges, the public relations and design consultancy with a good number of professional firms among its clients, says, there is so much good work around, you do not have to touch the dodgy stuff.

THE PROFESSIONS WAKE UP

The theory that the failings of business can be blamed on the low calibre of people in it holds a certain appeal. After all, the idea that business people are doers rather than thinkers helps explain why they seem to be such easy prey for the management gurus and consultants with their 'quick-fix', single-answer solutions to their problems.

But it cannot be correct. Yes, the people who join professional advisers are – in the main – more likely to be loaded with academic honours than those they end up assisting but, whether running parts of the Civil Service, law firms or advertising agencies, they seem no more adept at keeping the woes of business at bay than their counterparts at the heart of industry. Indeed, as we have seen, these people are so smart that they have developed an uncanny habit of picking up the habits of the organisations to which they are supposedly so superior at about the time when they are found to be wanting.

Moreover, do not forget that the people running the largest accountancy firms increasingly talk of what they do as an 'industry' and engage in the sorts of 'mega-mergers' that have become meat and drink to their clients, while those at the helm of advertising agencies and similar firms find it hard to resist the blandishments and share options proffered by the huge media corporations.

David Maister believes that for professionals to prosper they must be true to themselves. His latest book, *True Professionalism*, is essentially a call for lawyers, accountants, whoever, to believe passionately in what they do, never compromise their standards and values and care about their clients. If such 'core principles' sound obvious, it is not surprising. As Maister says, they are drawn from sound logic.

However, while Maister is highly regarded by the managers of some of the world's best-known firms, it is not clear that his words are always being taken to heart. With even middling-sized partnerships seemingly generally convinced that they need global reach in order to survive, it is easy to agree with his assessment that 'the prevailing ethos in many firms is "It's about the money, stupid!"' Nowhere is this more true than in foreign ventures. In their early years, in particular, they are frequently such a drain on resources that those embarked upon them often need income from anywhere they can get it just to keep their heads above water.

It can be argued that this need to generate work that brings hefty revenues just exacerbates the problem as Maister sees it: junior partners and those below them toiling away hour after hour because that is the way it has to be. His point is that it does not, or rather that it cannot.

Looking around at the ambitions of PricewaterhouseCoopers and at the problems besetting Andersen Worldwide, the organisation that was thought to have achieved the Holy Grail of a seamless international web of professional services of all sorts, you can see his point. Indeed, developments in the late 1990s within the accountancy profession in particular have probably hastened the ending of the concept of partnership as we know it. The simultaneous mergers and schisms among the leading firms demonstrate that managing global organisations in which thousands of people feel they can either influence what happens or ignore what they do not like is an impossibility.

Another thing that Maister successfully blows the gaff on is the idea put about by many people in professional services firms that being at the beck and call of ever-more-demanding clients is simply glorious fun. Basing his observations on his extensive contacts with firms around the world, he paints a very different picture. At 'one of the most profitable, elite law firms in the United States', he says, he asked the question, 'What percent of your clients would you put in the category of "I like these people"?' – to be met by gales of laughter. 'It became clear', he writes in a chapter headed 'Are You Having Fun Yet?', 'that many professionals do not *expect* to like their clients. The issue here is not an ethical or moral one (that you *should* like your clients and your work), but rather that it is *possible* to like (some of) them; and further that it is within every professional's power to influence which clients you work for, and what you do for them.'

The – very different – people at the fledgling advertising agency St Luke's and the accounting firm Rees Pollock know what he is talking about. Though they operate in two contrasting – and, in the view of many, diametrically opposed – fields, they have much more in common than might have been expected. Both are based in London and were born out of takeovers, but, more significantly, both exhibit a sense of purpose and a pride in what they are doing that would gladden the heart of Maister.

Moreover, both seem to share his suspicion of the idea that 'all new revenue is good revenue', a notion that, as we have seen, has been gaining rather wider currency of late. In the summer of 1997, for instance, St Luke's, which has from the start set its ethical heart of its sleeve by letting it be known it would not consider lucrative work on tobacco accounts, refused all new business on the grounds that it wanted to take stock after a period of fast growth. Meanwhile, Rees Pollock insists that it will refuse deals from which it stands to gain if it does not feel they are right for clients.

Rees Pollock began life in 1990, when Simon Rees and Andrew Pollock, along with a couple of partners who soon left after a dispute over direction, resigned from the then newly created firm of Ernst & Young on the grounds that they did not feel the new entity could serve their clients in growing businesses as well as they wanted.

Though the early disagreements with the now-departed partners and the deepest recession the south-east of England has ever known inevitably took their toll, in 1998 they were well established as a niche adviser to growing businesses. Growth had not been phenomenal – turnover was hovering around the £2 million mark, while the number of staff had crept up to about 25.

Then, however, as Richard Seymour, co-founder of the internationally renowned product designers Seymour Powell, says, turnover can be little more than vanity. The important thing – as both these firms, as well as St Luke's, have done – is to focus on doing good work that staff can feel proud of and enervated by.

Rees and Pollock, who were wise enough to leave Ernst & Young on sufficiently good terms that they use their old firm to train their staff and so keep up the quality, say that their reputation has risen to the point where they get 'quality people knocking on the door', while about 60 per cent of business is recurring work. Moreover, a good proportion of this work is made up of such appointments as investigations and litigation support, which generally require the approval of banks and other institutions.

Pollock himself has built a strong reputation in the area of franchises, advising such well-known names as Pirtek, a company that imported from Australia the idea of running a nationwide chain of mobile hydraulic hose installers and repairers, and the UK operations of Nevada Bob's, the US-based chain of golf shops.

Pollock says: 'This isn't about going out and selling. We do the selling when we do the work. The most important thing is to get a reputation for doing good work.'

> 'The most important thing is to get a reputation for doing good work.' – Andy Pollock of Rees Pollock.

Though he accepts that there might be a perception that in a world dominated by ever-growing large firms 'because we're small we can't be any good', he insists that the 'best sales force we have is our client base'. People who have seen the firm operate – often head-to-head with people from the biggest firms –use it again and again. Moreover, growing businesses know that the firm understands their problems because its staff have been through the process themselves.

Nevertheless, like Andy Law and David Abraham at St Luke's, they are wary of declaring that they have found any answers. Abraham terms the employee ownership at the highly rated young advertising agency an interesting 'experiment that is still successful' as if he wonders how long it can last, while Rees Pollock's Rees admits to concerns about not getting complacent as the firm gets older and feels more established through breaking out of the start-up phase. It is important to keep focused, he says.

Determined to remain cautious, even in the face of buoyant corporate activity, they insist that if the circumstances do not appear to be right they will advise clients against deals, although such decisions might mean losing fees in the short term. They feel that the longer-term benefits of having principles and of being of real help to clients who might otherwise become overexposed and thus collapse far outweigh any short-term disadvantages.

The same sort of thinking pervades St Luke's, where Abraham, who acts as chief operating officer to Law's chairman, says that the strategy is to 'grow only with very high-quality clients for whom we can do an excellent job and get paid fairly'. In its short history it has worked for such high-profile clients as Eurostar, the furniture maker Ikea and the UK Government's 'New Deal' programme to get the long-term employed back to work. Though many in its highly competitive industry doubted whether breaking with the old model would work, the agency has won many plaudits and is noted for the creativity it brings to its campaigns.

This emphasis on good work is partly designed to avoid falling into the trap Maister talks of when he says that not all revenue is good revenue. As Abraham points out, a lot of professional services firms are tempted to build client lists. This might be because they think that they have to keep their people busy or it might be because they have expensive premises. Whatever, it is not the sort of policy that is going to bring out the best in people and encourage them to reach for their highest standards. Instead, they are more likely to devise ways of ensuring that they can do the minimum required to deal with all the work coming their way.

> *Building up client lists is not the sort of policy that is going to bring out the best in people and encourage them to reach for their highest standards.*

Abraham's attitude is that 'you can't tell people to work on something that they don't want to'. But he points out that the other side of this is that when people are really interested in an account they will work really hard to get it – his explanation for what he claims is the agency's extraordinarily high success rate in pitches. While the industry average is to win about one in five of the pitches you attend, St Luke's is successful in about 60 per cent, he says.

Of course, there is a particular reason why in his case he does not feel he can tell people to do something they do not want to: everybody who works there has a share in the business, and hence a say in how it is run.

The agency – named for the patron saint of creative people – was formed as a result of the October 1995 breakaway from Chiat Day, itself renowned for experimenting with unusual management methods and accommodation. Indeed, Law and some colleagues had started developing some of the ideas behind St Luke's when it was still the London office of Chiat Day, but the company was sold to Omnicom just as they were about to be put into practice. Law, then managing director of the London operation, refused to go along with the deal and invited everybody in the office to join him in leaving. Once they had done that, he has said, they got rid of the greed and envy that is endemic not just in advertising but also in a range of other industries.

Things have moved on rapidly. For a start, the original staff of 25 had nearly trebled, to 100, by the summer of 1998. And that had led to other changes, especially in the way the organisation is managed. But the organisation, based close to London's Euston railway station, remains wedded to the notion of employee-ownership.

Law and Abraham's initial instinct was to do little formal management, but even the consultants from the social auditing specialist SustainAbility told them that the place needed leadership. 'We came to a conclusion about the role of management,' says Abraham. 'Not to be embarrassed about it, but not to do it in the old way.' Accordingly, the agency has adopted an almost HP-style system of self-managed groups supported by taskforces that tackle specific issues.

For instance, concerns about how people joining the agency were treated has led to the setting up of a group dedicated to working out ways of improving that, while another is looking at the future use of technology.

> 'A shareholding is just a piece of paper. You have to be able to translate that into a sense of ownership.' – David Abraham of St Luke's.

All the time, however, Abraham and Law are looking to get people more involved in the running of the place. 'A shareholding is just a piece of paper.

You have to be able to translate that into a sense of owner-ship,' says Abraham.

Though Law and Abraham insist that the ownership struc-ture is central to what their organisation has achieved, it is not the end of the story. There is at St Luke's – in the decision to be based outside of the 'media village' of London's Soho, in the building of 'account rooms' in the style of the product or or-ganisation that is the subject of the work and, of course, in the decision not to be named after a series of account or creative directors – a sense of purpose that goes beyond the sort of interest that comes from having a share of the business. After all, it is not every law or accountancy firm where the partners are so obviously enjoying and proud of what they do.

Now, this could partly be the business. Many veterans talk of the fun they still have, while – in the related field of design – the fun that product designers Richard Seymour and Dick Powell have in working out new ways of building flawed prod-ucts is palpable from any of the television programmes in which they have starred. As one reviewer said, they instil a sense of enjoyment in business that is rarely apparent.

But there is something special about St Luke's. With only one person leaving from the original 35 in the first year of operation, there is plenty of evidence that the model is attrac-tive. It helps that the worker's co-operative model has been modified to allow competitive salaries to be paid for star peo-ple.

Such is the fledgling organisation's reputation that people who have heard of it in several far-flung countries have been hired. 'We've got people from Sweden and America,' says Abraham. 'People are hearing about us and knocking on the door.'

What keeps them around is that they are motivated to stand for something. St Luke's passes up large fees by refusing to work on tobacco accounts, while – though wary of becoming too 'PC' and getting away from the irreverent spirit of advertising – to a certain extent it screens the ethical policies of would-be clients. 'Integrity is what motivates people', Abraham adds. 'People want to work hard, but not for organisations that they feel are letting them down.'

In other words, they need to be engaged. And once that happens, everything becomes a lot simpler and Law can set an unattainable vision confident that people will nevertheless strive to reach it.

Neither Abraham nor Law claims that their experiment is trouble-free, but they are themselves sufficiently enthused about what they see as a new approach to work to be spreading the gospel. The New Deal work was eagerly undertaken, for example, because it was seen as a great opportunity to 'preach to the rest of the world about [business's] broader responsibilities'.

Law's own particular mission is to change 'the DNA of business' so that companies get back to the idea that it 'exists for people' rather than purely to maximise shareholder returns.

Contrast that, not just with Travers Smith Braithwaite, but with many other firms. In going for growth at seemingly any cost, they appear to forget that the 'people' by whom they set such store have emotions that will be engaged by work – and clients – that they believe in. It is easy for firms to claim that they have systems in place to prevent them getting caught out by rogue or simply over-ambitious clients. But the stories of many of the corporate collapses of the late 1980s featured many well-known advisers who seemed unaware of certain facets of their clients' activities that were known to others.

Firms should not be surprised that if they repeat this approach in the years ahead they will fall in the estimation of not just the outside world but also their own employees. There is nothing like setting – and living up to – high ethical standards to make a workforce feel good about itself.

In other words, integrity is a key component in creating the sense of engagement that sets one organisation apart from another, making it more likely to succeed in the longer term.

Chapter 6

SHOW SOME RESPECT

The arrival of ever cheaper and more powerful information technology has in the mid to late 1990s played a formidable part in the creation of another business myth to add to the hundreds described by the likes of the business writer William Davis. This is the notion that, if you set up a system that rewards people for returning to your shop, they will fall into line and do as bidden.

It did not take long, of course, for 'loyalty cards' – as this concept has become known – to be renamed 'promiscuity cards' – for the simple reason that they do not engender loyalty. Yes, consumers collect the points, just as they do the air miles and the tokens from service stations. But there is little sign that they alter their behaviour significantly as a result.

Indeed, one of the fields in which loyalty cards are used most intensively is supermarket retailing. But such shopping is largely a matter of habit. Even though Britain, in particular, has seen what seems like an explosion in the number of supermarkets, consumers will often have little choice between retailers unless they want to go a long way out of their way.

If they do decide to change, they receive another loyalty card – which it is possible to run in tandem with the existing one. So, where is the loyalty? How does a consumer lose by abandoning the organisation that issued the card and joining up with a fresh one?

In other words, loyalty cards are a reasonably effective way for a retailer to track what sorts of goods its customers favour and, accordingly, stock its stores appropriately (always assuming that its equipment and software are sufficiently sophisticated), but they are not in themselves a source of what today is known as 'competitive advantage'. If everybody has them, how can they be?

> *Loyalty cards are a reasonably effective way for a retailer to track what sorts of goods its customers favour and, accordingly, stock its stores appropriately, but they are not in themselves a source of what today is known as 'competitive advantage'.*

Consequently, if in Britain Tesco has stolen a march on Sainsbury, it is probably a lot more to do with a range of management issues rather than one tool. At a time when Sainsbury, still showing the signs of being something of a family company, was basking in its reputation as the middle-class's favoured supermarket, Tesco was apparently hungrier. Keen to cast off its old 'pile 'em high, sell 'em cheap' image, it was more alert to changes in shoppers' habits, quick to see that quality and value for money were not incompatible and realised that it was no good the top management setting out plans if those further down the organisation did not feel able to carry them out. Consequently, the company seems to have mastered a trick usually associated with the likes of HP and other high-tech companies, of having people at all levels understanding what is required of them and being prepared to do things on their own initiative, rather than always being reactive.

Hence, it can be seen that, just as Wal-Mart in the USA is much more than just a low-cost chain, so Tesco has fought the battle for control of the supermarket turf on many fronts.

Similarly, though value for money are hallmarks of both Marks & Spencer and the John Lewis Partnership, these two British stores groups do not owe all their success to that. It cannot be a coincidence that – while other parts of the retail sector see their fortunes ebb and flow, even within supposed periods of economic prosperity – they report almost continuous expansion. After all, the similarities do not end there.

Both are noted for quality as well as price and both clearly invest in their people. M&S may have abandoned certain aspects of its paternalistic culture over the years, but working for the company is still a better bet for security than signing up for most retailers, which are perhaps most extremely affected by the boom-and-bust business cycle to which Britain seems wedded. For the John Lewis Partnership, the connection is all the more apparent because – as the group's name suggests – employees have a significant stake in the business.

The 'partners' perhaps lack the total dedication to customer service that is the hallmark of the best US organisations, notably the Gap and that management guru's favourite, Nordstrom. But in Britain regular customers of the shops in this chain swear by the service and helpfulness of the staff – almost taking it for granted, until they go elsewhere.

Few areas of management have in recent years been so productive for gurus and other consultants as customer service. And yet, so many organisations are still to be found wanting.

John Lewis's chairman, Sir Stuart Hampson, is in no doubt why the organisation he heads has done so well. The people who deal with the public – whether sales assistants, managers or delivery van drivers – have a much greater than usual desire to make the customer happy because they are valued as employees and have a realistic prospect of long-term employment.

Hampson even entitled a speech delivered to the RSA's forum for ethics in the workplace in February 1998 'I like being an employee'. His point was that all the talk of the previous few years of regular employment becoming a thing of the past, with 'virtual organisations' becoming the norm and individuals adopting 'portfolio careers' had been somewhat overdone.

'This might be an image of a brave new world, but I don't believe it's what the majority of people want. I also don't believe that it is a recipe for commercial success or for social harmony,' he told his audience.

> *'I don't believe it's what the majority of people want. I also don't believe that it is a recipe for commercial success or for social harmony.' – Sir Stuart Hampson of the John Lewis Partnership on 'portfolio careers'.*

'I have no difficulty in accepting the need for more flexible styles of working. The danger is that this approach is seized on by those who are keen to exalt the primacy of the shareholder and espouse any theory which will focus more sharply on the economic purpose of companies,' he added, before quoting from one of an abundant crop of shareholder value books as evidence of 'the ruthless search for efficiency rather than relationships'.

Encouraging people to see a business merely as 'an investment project, brought into existence to earn in excess of its cost of capital' (as Shiv Mathur and Alfred Kenyon put it in *Creating Value*) was not a viewpoint he shared. Such an approach amounts to exploiting human resources, he said. But then there are some who say that the replacement of the term 'personnel' with 'human resources' might have made the discipline sound grander, but it demonstrated that people were assets like any other.

At any rate, Hampson, who has gone on to combine running the retail group with being chairman of the Centre for Tomorrow's Company, a think-tank designed to promote the concept of stakeholding, or the 'inclusive approach', said he was 'firmly convinced that companies who do not fully respect their relationship with their employees are missing out on a powerful driver to business advantage'.

Companies, he pointed out, often insisted that their competitive advantage came from their commitment to their customers – their ability to understand what customers wanted, to adapt their product to match expectations. 'But who's doing the understanding? Who's doing the adapting?' he asked in an echo of the thinking of Rosenbluth, the Pennsylvania-based international travel company that makes a point of putting the customers second – on the basis that they can only receive top-level service if the company's employees are happy.

Drawing on the notion developed by Charles Handy, the management guru who is himself a portfolio worker, that there were companies made up of 'citizens' – rather than the more usual mercenaries – who were people that felt proud to be part of the company, he said: 'I don't see how an efficient army of engaged citizens can be raised on a short-term basis.' While individual talent might be high, 'commitment will never be the same as for someone who has spent time coming to know a company and its values, who identifies their personal future with the company's future.'

Accepting that there will be exceptions to the model of hundreds of employees retained on a full-time basis – notably, companies such as the sports shoe and clothing maker Nike, which is mostly a marketing operation that buys in manufacturing, design and the rest as and when it is needed – he nevertheless believes that most employees are looking for more than just a job.

'They are looking to identify with the value of their work. They want to feel pride in what they do, to feel that they are working for a company they admire and respect, to sense that their contribution to the business is both real and recognised,' he says, stressing that any company not tapping into such enthusiasm is putting itself at a significant disadvantage. 'It is a basic human instinct to identify with something to which you devote your energy, your enthusiasm – and feeling pride in the achievements of your company should be as natural as supporting the local football team.'

As he points out, employees are not likely to feel that sort of involvement with the sort of financially driven vehicles advocated by many gurus. It is all very well talking about incentivising people, but – for all the sophistication being introduced to the models – it is very hard to engage those down the organisation about something as nebulous as shareholder value.

Senior executives will get it, of course, since they can see the effect directly in their pay packets. But for most people more than financial motivation is important. At Nucor Steel, for example, it would be easy to assume that the bonuses paid to all staff are entirely responsible for the company's success. In fact, though, they are only a part of it – indeed, they can be seen as merely the result of enabling people to see work as a worthwhile activity in which notions of 'them and us' are abandoned in the quest to do business.

As Hampson says, 'people look for a company's values, for its soul, and then they can begin to believe in it.' Though this might sound like a return to the sort of paternalism favoured by the Victorians, he is at pains to point out that it is in effect really a 'free election to support a company's character, which brings satisfaction and fulfilment to the employee as much as advantage to the employer.'

> *Companies are successful, particularly where, as in retail, they require the majority of their employees to deal with customers if they can create a situation in which both they and the people working for them share a common purpose.*

This seems to be the crux of the matter – companies are successful, particularly where, as in retail, they require the majority of their employees to deal with customers if they can create a situation in which both they and the people working for them share a common purpose. And when there is such a purpose, as at the likes of 3M, HP and Nucor, self-confidence is not likely to be far away.

Outsiders obtain a lot of amusement from the *The Gazette*, the John Lewis Partnership's weekly in-house magazine, because of the often coded criticisms of the organisation that appear in the letters page. Equally, many were amazed to believe

that the organisation would have approved a television programme about the group that at times featured employees being less than glowing about their jobs. But these are classic
signs of self-confidence. Organisations that are seriously worried about a lack of internal 'buy in' to what they are doing are
likely to be much more guarded about such matters.

The problem for anybody wishing to emulate this sort of
thing is that it takes a long time. Self-confidence and the other
qualities of like-minded organisations, such as mutual respect,
loyalty and commitment, cannot be acquired in the twinkling
of an eye. They are not tools or techniques in the conventional
sense because they only work if genuinely adhered to and held
dear for significant lengths of time.

As with 3M and HP, the John Lewis Partnership abides by
principles set out a long time ago, in this case by the company's
founder. According to the potted version of his words set out
on the back page of *The Gazette* every week, 'the partnership's
supreme purpose is to secure the fairest possible sharing by all
its members of the advantages of ownership – gain, knowledge
and power; that is to say, their happiness in the broadest sense
of the word so far as happiness depends upon gainful occupation'.

Making this happen produces what Hampson calls 'an interesting three-way stretch'. If the company makes a profit, it
distributes it to its partners, since it has no outside shareholders. But if the only way to make a profit was to make partners
redundant it could hardly claim to be contributing to partners'
happiness. And yet if it is too lenient in the treatment of staff it
will lose out in the harsh competitive environment that has
become a particular feature of retailing. It is, as he says, 'a
good test of management'.

However, it appears to be one that many organisations are
unwilling to take. Companies talk a lot about ideas like loyalty
and commitment, but they do not mean them to be the

foundations for a genuine shared purpose; for many, they are just another couple of concepts that sound good but should not be taken too far.

Companies talk a lot about ideas like loyalty and commitment, but they do not mean them to be the foundations for a genuine shared purpose; for many, they are just another couple of concepts that sound good but should not be taken too far.

Given that, it is hardly surprising when cynicism seeps in – especially when members of the workforce see senior executives apparently being rewarded for not doing what they are extolling others to do. Commitment and loyalty are not always reciprocated. How many times have senior executives suddenly left organisations, often when they are in the midst of some upheaval?

This could certainly be said to be the case with WH Smith, when Bill Cockburn – who had recently joined from the Post Office – left to become managing director of BT in the run-up to its planned merger with MCI. Though the board of Smith might have garnered some pleasure from the fact that the deal subsequently foundered, they could not have been amused by the fact that their attempts to turnaround an ailing high-street giant were being hampered in this way.

Certainly, they would receive the sympathy of Hampson, who takes the attitude that 'leadership is long-term'. Though senior managers may be fired if they fail to do what is expected of them, they need to understand that being made a director or especially chief executive entails commitment. 'In my book, whatever the contract says, a chief executive cannot simply walk out because a better offer comes along.'

And look how the principles of commitment and loyalty work at John Lewis when applied to employees. In 1990, the group decided to close down two of its smaller stores, one in a declining area of south London and the other in a similar district in the north of the capital. With each shop employing about 400 people, the board delayed closure until the opening of a new store in another part of London was imminent. Because this development would lead to various staff moves around the

London stores as well as the creation of new vacancies, the company undertook that everyone working in the two closed shops would be offered jobs in various branches. But then came the recession and a sharp downturn in retailing. However, the company kept its word – and 12 months later was still carrying 100 people above what it needed.

Hampson accepts that some might say that was fine for John Lewis since it could afford the gesture (though he did not add that plenty of other organisations that could afford it just as well if not better do not follow suit). He also takes the point that the partnership constitution requires such action. But he responds by pointing to the costs of *not* acting in this way.

As a result of the loyalty and commitment shown by the business, the confidence of employees has been enhanced. 'If any of them have an idea for improving the efficiency of the business, even if it means the collapse of their job, they can bring that idea forward without fear.' says Hampson. 'The threat of unemployment is inimical to flexibility: people hold on to what they are doing, instead of moving to what they could do best, what they enjoy most, what would contribute most to the success of the company.'

THE END OF TRUST

Contrast this with the world of cynicism in which employees at all levels – but especially middle managers – are tired of hearing senior executives say one thing but do another, are fed up of having to implement initiative after initiative and have pretty much lost their commitment to the organisations they serve.

At a time when loyalty – or the lack of it on the part of organisations and, more recently, those who work in them – is under constant discussion, it is being realised that respect and trust are commodities that are in very short supply. Companies like HP, 3M and WL Gore Associates, the maker of precision medical products as well as that mysterious weather-beating substance Gore-Tex, where there are no job titles, all obviously have respect for their employees and for the larger community.

However, this is not universally the case. As Eileen Shapiro, debunker of management myths, points out, there is a terrible tendency for those in the higher echelons of business to act and speak as if they think everybody else is stupid.

It is, she says, 'some kind of elitism' that comes in when people reach positions of power. Whether they apply this approach to employees or customers makes no difference; it saps the energy of those working there.

If, for example, a senior executive abandons the questioning side to their nature he or she was known to have on the way up and acts as if there is no chance that there is anybody in the organisation less than totally ecstatic about being there, the result is likely to be heightened cynicism, combined with disdain, among employees.

Organisations can only achieve total 'buy-in' from their employees if they offer them some kind of role in the decision-making process – especially at a time when the quality of decision-making is seen as so important that organisations are actively encouraged to lift every stone in the search for the answers. If the idea or solution that management is seeking to impose on a workforce is generally reckoned to be seriously flawed, the chances of take-up of this kind are limited.

Equally, if an executive is prepared to settle for mediocre quality in the goods or services that his or her organisation is producing, it is the customers who are considered gullible. As long as the goods or services are well packaged, they will know no difference, or so goes this line of thinking. One venture capitalist was so aghast at hearing the managing director of a company in which he had invested respond to a question about quality with the remark, 'It's all right' that he immediately set about finding a replacement.

Quite apart from giving the business concerned only limited chances of success when quality is almost a given, this is a strategy with the capacity to corrupt a whole organisation. As Shapiro points out, the things an organisation has to do to reinforce that message – such as hiring people who are not as good as the top management – are liable to turn off the employees to such an extent that they have very little value.

People are likely to perform better if they are expected to achieve a lot rather than if they are told not to try too hard. Employers who take the 'least that we can get away with' approach ought to bear in mind that pride in what you are doing is a great motivator. But even those who do not deliberately aim low can still have a problem with trust. If use of the word 'trust' is on the rise in management circles it is largely because of the perceived lack of it.

> *If use of the word 'trust' is on the rise in management circles it is largely because of the perceived lack of it.*

A business environment in which short-term pressures seem to take precedence over long-term ambition has not just spawned a 'hire 'em, fire 'em' approach to people management; that is only the beginning. Management might have started off in the driving seat when, at the start of this decade, it used the powerful combination of recession, the enthusiasm for the then new management concept of re-engineering and anxiety about the coming millennium to change the rules of employment. But the ending of the so-called psychological contract under which employees expected a certain amount of job security in return for their loyalty, and its replacement by what was termed 'flexibility' but which was in fact often longer hours and greater responsibility for little extra reward, led to what was probably an unexpected response in the workforce.

While many employees have either lost their jobs or been forced to work under increasingly stressful conditions, many others have recognised their value to organisations and – seizing on the new freedoms – set themselves up as consultants, contractors or whatever and offered their services to the highest bidder or to those for which they really want to work.

The result is a kind of free-for-all in which, thanks to the vogue for outsourcing and temporary employees, it is often difficult to see where one organisation begins and another ends.

It is this situation that Peter Herriot, one of the first researchers to write about the 'new deal' in the employment market, and two colleagues at Sussex University's Institute of Employment Studies explore in their book *Trust and Transition*. Subtitled *Managing Today's Employment Relationship*, it argues that senior executives face an acute dilemma: 'How can we innovate into new markets, services and products when we have destroyed over the last two decades, but especially over the last five years, the conditions necessary to do so?'

Senior executives face an acute dilemma: 'How can we innovate into new markets, services and products when we have destroyed over the last two decades, but especially over the last five years, the conditions necessary to do so?'

Innovation, point out Herriot, Wendy Hirsh and Peter Reilly, needs a willingness to take risks, and therefore a degree of psychological security. It also needs employees to have agency and autonomy, or the sense that what they do affects outcomes and that they can decide what action to take. And, while ideas often come to individuals on their own, teamworking is often required to bring those ideas to fruition.

Yet, they add, 'in our desire to cut costs, we have reduced these very conditions to breaking point. By downsizing, we have reduced employees' sense of security. By setting tight budget targets and reducing resources we have decreased agency and autonomy, despite all the rhetoric of empowerment. And by concentrating on motivating individuals by performance-related pay, we have shown what little value we place on teamwork.'

Nor are they the only ones to take this view. A 1997 survey by management consultants at Coopers & Lybrand came to the conclusion that the key to high performance in innovation was trust. Moreover, some of the companies that have the strongest records in this area make a point of placing their trust in employees. In place of the old command-and-control attitudes, their executives set general guidelines and – taking the view that most people have sufficient pride in what they are doing not to mess around wilfully at work – let their workforces get on with the tasks set them.

And in his book *The Trust Effect*, consultant Larry Reynolds argues that 'not only is trust the key issue for business, but business is trusted less than ever before'.

Trust, says Reynolds, is about relationships. In fact, it is just one of three basic ways of conducting a relationship. The other two are based on power – the typical command-and-control set-up – and hope – where, in yet another manifestation of the either/or mentality so prevalent in business, those that feel that power has not worked opt for abandoning all controls and going for 'empowerment'. Reynolds makes clear that he feels this can be worse than the former because it allows people's spirits to be raised only to be dashed.

Trust, on the other hand, is based on people doing things, 'not because they have to, not because they hope it will do them good in the end, but because they genuinely want to.' And they want to because on one level they are confident that the organisation is genuinely concerned about them and on another because they identify closely with its values and be-liefs.

Reynolds is also at pains to point out that this is no easy street. Trust works, he says, because it brings accountability. People are expected to meet certain targets and if they fail they typically receive coaching aimed at bringing about an improve-ment or they are ushered out of the organisation. 'Trust is tough,' he says.

He cites the US retailer Nordstrom as strong on trust. With committed customers ranging from former Ford chairman Donald Peterson to the management guru Tom Peters, the company certainly has a great reputation. And by common consent that is down to its attitude towards its staff – its employee handbook apparently says little more than 'use your good judgement in all situations'. HP is another that falls into this category, as is Starbucks, the Seattle-based gourmet coffee company that inspired and then took over the British-based operator, Seattle Coffee Company.

But there are not legions of others in this situation. Organisations' typical responses to the changing employment relationship have tended to 'decrease further the already diminished social capital available to them. They have lost the trust of their employees. A pervasive insecurity among employees throws further into jeopardy what little trust is still around.'

Nor is it just employees whose trust they have lost; customers, too, no longer trust many of the organisations with which they carry out transactions. After all, Richard Branson's Virgin has only been able to make the in-roads it has on the British financial services industry because of the general distrust of the sector. A situation that has only been exacerbated by the pensions mis-selling scandal.

But, bleak as the picture is, Herriot and his colleagues believe that trust can be recreated – largely through senior managers abandoning their lofty perches and going at least some way towards empathising with employees' predicaments. That, though, demands a different style of leadership to the one with which most organisations are familiar.

WHERE WE GO FROM HERE

Things *are* changing. The vocabulary is adapting to a new world in which such concepts as social auditing, environmental reporting and ethics codes are moving from the fringes towards the mainstream, while the idea that other groups beyond managers and shareholders have an interest in the success or otherwise of a business is suddenly regarded as beyond argument.

However, so far there has been more talk than action. The US corporate model still holds sway to such an extent that there are still some organisations and business leaders for whom the aim of business is purely and simply to make a profit. And they are apt to take the current enthusiasm for the admittedly powerful notion of value creation being the greatest test of performance as proving their point – even though, as has been explained in this book, this is much better achieved by breaking into new fields than by seeking to suck cost out of existing operations.

Now, it is possible to argue that there is nothing wrong with that, per se. It is, we are told, all part of the way in which financial markets work – redistribution of capital, the drive

for efficient use of funds, etc. And it is an even more fundamental part of the buyout market – which has been booming
in the mid to late 1990s, incidentally – where investors are said
to have at least one eye on their exit even before they have
started.

However, this drive for cash is starting to cause concern
throughout the developed world. Of course, some of those voicing such worries are those who have always disapproved of
markets and are, by nature, opposed to everything that business does. They want some kind of social nirvana where every
business person is a model citizen giving generously to charity,
paying well above the minimum wage and never laying people
off.

Yet, more and more consultants and executives are talking
about the keys to success being based around such 'soft' issues
as passion, trust, purpose, values and integrity. All of these are
fine words that – if the rhetoric accords with the experiences of
employees, customers and other members of the stakeholder
society – can genuinely inspire.

The problem is that, in the vast majority of cases, they are
seen as part of the picture. It is rather as if they are still seen as
the sort of 'nice' things that can happen if you have got in place
the right systems and techniques for creating innovation or a
focus on value creation. In fact, though, there is growing evidence to suggest that it is the other way around. Innovation
and value creation occur most effectively in organisations characterised by such emotions as trust and passion.

For example, Trevor Davis, a former research metallurgist
who became a consultant with PricewaterhouseCoopers, points
to how these notions are high up on the agendas of both the
high-performing companies in his 1997 innovation survey and
in the examination of high-growth companies conducted by
his firm in conjunction with Templeton College, Oxford and
Virgin. Significantly, the findings accord pretty much with research conducted among leading fast-growing private compa-

nies identified in a eight-year study conducted by the *Independent on Sunday* and accountants at the former Price Waterhouse.

The changes are apparent in the story of Camelot and the National Lottery, a sort of parable for our times. Now, of course, the difference in attitude – from the 'this is a business like any other and people have got to be given incentives to do a good job' line to the more ameliorative 'well, it might be possible to look at ways of doing it on a non-profit-making basis' stance of just a few months later – is at least partly attributable to actions and words from culture secretary Chris Smith and others in Tony Blair's government.

However, that set of ministers has been more than usually well-attuned to popular sentiment, and – whatever the logic of a situation where people are driven by greed to spend millions of pounds a week on a lottery yet accuse those that run the affair of showing the same characteristic – there was a sense in the few months around the middle of 1997 that Camelot had lost what the Tomorrow's Company people might call 'the licence to operate'.

In continually being at odds with the Government over the levels of profits and bonuses, the directors were demonstrating that they had not realised the extent to which the climate had changed. The new government's policies might not have been markedly different, but people's expectations of what life would be like had. Accordingly, it was paramount for prominent organisations of this kind to improve their behaviour.

Progress was initially slow. At first, the organisation – a consortium formed by the British companies Racal, De La Rue, Cadbury Schweppes, ICL and the controversial US-based lottery organiser GTech – suggested that directors might resign if ordered by Smith to repay bonuses. But in the end a compromise was reached under which secret donations to charity were made.

Time will tell whether the British people will learn to love Camelot as much as they love the thought that some of them could gain a share of the jackpot. But the comparatively rapid shift in their stance from the original 'What's all the fuss about?' line to the departure of G-Tech from the list of shareholders in the consortium, in the wake of Richard Branson's libel victory in the bribery scandal, is indicative of a realisation by the organisation's PR advisers at least that times had changed. Significantly, the first results announcement following the public outcry prompted by directors' pay rising as profits and payments to good causes fell met with no anger. Instead, the organisation quietly announced plans to hand over an extra £1 billion to good causes as it reported a 10 per cent rise in profits.

Meanwhile, increasing numbers of companies around the world are realising that survival in the 21st century is going to require adherence to a new

> *Increasing numbers of companies around the world are realising that survival in the 21st century is going to require adherence to a new set of principles, or rules of engagement.*

set of principles, or rules of engagement. This is not to say that rigidly following a single approach will do the trick; the strength of the principles behind HP or 3M is that they provide guidance rather than answers and so enable whoever is leading the company at a given time to make shifts into new markets or in management style, confident in the knowledge that such moves are not leading in inappropriate directions.

Nor is it to say that lots of touchy-feeliness is required either. As the managers responsible for the Co-operative Bank's decision to up the ante in the social auditing arena with the publication of a 'partnership report' point out, such initiatives are not alternatives to conventional methods of reporting; they are part and parcel of a better way of understanding business performance. Indeed, the bank attributes its marked rise in 1997 profits to its ethical stance.

Just as companies renowned for innovation are said to have 'tight–loose' systems of control, so those genuinely concerned to measure their achievements in the round are also steely in their attentiveness to traditional financial measures. But beyond the great societal issues that companies such as Body Shop, Ben & Jerry's Ice Cream and the Co-operative Bank have realised have the power to engage us, there is an opportunity for organisations to win over hearts and minds at the individual level.

Technology has great potential to rid workers of many of their frustrations – increasingly, thanks to laptop computers, modems and fax machines, it is possible to meet client or customer deadlines and get to your child's sports day.

Similarly, some organisations and consultancies are going to great lengths to explore what the modern office should really look like. The advertising agency St Luke's has done its bit in this regard with its special rooms and free-roaming staff, and there are signs – from a PA Consulting report – that such thinking is starting to spread beyond the realm of the 'creative' industries.

Obviously, it is up to the most senior executives to make employees, customers and suppliers feel good about the organisation by making the right sorts of products, selling them in the right sort of way and generally setting the tone. But the sort of thing that really fires up employees, makes them talk about the company they work for in the 'us' and 'we' terms as they use for their favourite sports team, is what happens at the coalface.

> *The sort of thing that really fires up employees, makes them talk about the company they work for in the same 'us' and 'we' terms as they use for their favourite sports team, is what happens at the coalface.*

Tom Peters would call it the 'Wow Factor'. Others might describe it as 'pride in your work'. You might refer to it as 'You'd tell your mates down the pub'. Whatever, it is where managers come in – and where hitherto they have failed us.

In organisations that understand the rules of engagement, middle managers are not hapless overheads despised in equal measure by cost-cutting chief executives and long-suffering employees. They do not fill their days with the sort of senseless tedium that characterises the 'Dilbert' comic strip. No, they make a difference.

All the studies of new ways of working – from teleworking and homeworking, via hotelling to operating in virtual teams – indicate that there are tremendous challenges to management involved. And when they talk about management, they do not just mean senior executives, though they can do a lot to set the tone. They also mean middle managers – because they are the ones who in the organisations of the 21st century will be charged with producing results.

In the increasingly dispersed operations that make up to-day's more successful enterprises, most people have hardly heard of the senior executives, so it falls to those responsible for these individual business units to get the best out of employees. They can draw on the responsibility and freedom given to them by largely absent senior executives to give similar opportunities to those working with rather than for them.

On the basis that the only test should be the business case, middle managers can increase the chances of their own survival as well as that of the organisations they have often worked on behalf of for so long if they take the initiative in making work a happier and thus more productive place. Now that the ground has been prepared through changes in industrial relations and in putting business more squarely at the centre of society, it is a challenge to which they must rise.

The marketing world is doing its bit by talking about aligning brands and corporate reputation or integrity. Though even some of their number worry that this will lead to such notions being hijacked in the name of selling a few more cornflakes, cans of instant coffee, cars or whatever, it is an important issue at a time when the sheer amount of competition means that companies cannot rely on just selling more products; they must also sell themselves.

An additional challenge arises from the fact that, even as they are seeking to differentiate themselves from their competitors, organisations are going to have to do this more subtly than has been the case in the mid to late 1990s.

Though one setback does not necessarily indicate a trend, it is nevertheless possible to see the losses reported by Nike in mid-1998 as a sign that that sort of aggressive selling might have had its day.

Much had been made of the fact that the company is in reality a 'virtual organisation' that has as its chief function marketing. But then it became a received view that maybe the product itself was virtual, amounting to a logo or slogan that, by virtue of its association first with the basketball star Michael Jordan and then with all kinds of other highly rated sports performers, was desirable. Even the hefty prices seemed to increase the allure.

However, 'in your face' as the advertising was, it could be argued that it did not really stand for the sorts of things that people wanted in the late 1990s. It was really just hollow posturing, made worse, of course, if those featured in the commercials failed to live up to their over-the-top billing.

If it is increasingly true that marketing is now too important to be left to the marketing department and that human resources strategy cannot be consigned to the human resources department, it is certainly the case that leadership has outgrown the traditional leadership cadre. In increasing numbers of businesses increasing numbers of people are becoming leaders.

This requires a new approach to leadership. In particular, there is a need for British companies to adopt some of the thinking of their European counterparts and challenge the US notion of the chief executive as demi-god – as epitomised by all those cover stories in *Fortune* and *Business Week* magazines.

It is, after all, becoming increasingly true that, while we stick to the traditional view of 'political leaders', 'business leaders' and the rest, the net of leadership is widening. In organisations, the advent of empowerment and flatter structures means that, in effect, we are all leaders now. In sports, too, it is becoming more common for team captains to tell interviewers that a win was not solely down to them, but to the 11, 15 or however many leaders out there that day.

> *Leadership has outgrown the traditional leadership cadre. In increasing numbers of businesses increasing numbers of people are becoming leaders.*

To see this in action, one only has to look at a company such as AES Corporation, a Virginia-based power-generating company that has attracted a lot of attention because of the extent to which it has devolved power and decision-making to employees.

A *Wall Street Journal* article of July 1995, referred to in John Case's book *The Open-Book Management Experience*, described how a 'cash-investments task force' comprising plant technicians was put in charge of investing the money in the company's Connecticut plant's reserve fund. Charged with putting the money in various forms of debt instruments, the employees were given a basic course in finance and left to get on with the job. As Case writes: 'They investigated interest rates. They placed the buy-and-sell calls to brokers each week. They made the decisions.'

Nor was this the only way in which important tasks – previously the preserve of management – were devolved. An article in the February–March 1998 issue of *Fast Company* described how the company extended the principles developed in the USA to its operations overseas. For example, a chemical engineer two years into his first job in the power industry was given sole responsibility for negotiating a deal in Brazil on the basis that he had experience of a difficult partnership and therefore might know what made them work.

It is all part of a business philosophy developed by the company's founders, Dennis Bakke and Roger Sant. Bakke told *Fast Company* that 'we all want to be part of a community and to use our skills to make a difference in the world', while Sant's view is that taking this kind of approach had enabled the company to grow from fewer than 600 people in 1993 to nearly 10 times as many five years later. 'People would bring deals for us to approve, and we would have a huge bottleneck. We've shifted to giving advice rather than giving approval. And we've moved ahead much faster than we would have otherwise.'

Nevertheless, such attitudes bring complexities. And it is in an attempt to explain such confusion that Bill Drath, a research scientist at the Center for Creative Leadership in the USA, is developing a notion he terms 'relational leadership'. Essentially, this is a challenge to the longstanding assumption that leadership is all about individuals and – because leadership is a quality of a person or a process that flows from a person – how they can influence or head a group. The concept being developed by Drath and colleagues at the North Carolina-based research and training organisation suggests that leadership might be better understood as a collective phenomenon or 'the property of a social system'.

He points out that 'leadership is in some ways one of the most individual ideas that people invented'. After all, 'most talk of leadership starts with talk of *the leader*.' But he questions whether this is the most effective way to describe the reality, especially when the trend for globalisation is creating a need 'to be different and to be together at the same time'.

With mission statements and values all the rage, even the latest management thinking makes one of the key roles of leadership creating a vision on the basis, says Drath, that a single individual's 'moral, ethical or strategic sense of the world' will enlist others in the cause. But he questions this view of the leader as some kind of all-knowing scientist.

Instead, there is a need to 'develop theories of leadership of making sense of what we are doing'. If we look upon leadership in this way, leaders become part of the process, but not the leaders of it. 'The CEO is not causing that process any more than I am', he adds.

> *Leaders become part of the process, but not the leaders of it.*

It is hard to argue with the notion that looking at the idea of leadership in this way provides a better understanding of why – in politics, in particular – there is a perception that certain times require certain types of leader. For example, the past two decades have seen Margaret Thatcher and Tony Blair, two very different types of leader, in style at least, enjoy election landslides. Further back, Winston Churchill was the hero of World War II but was unceremoniously dumped in favour of Clement Atlee when it was felt that the peace called for a different personality.

Moreover, the idea that the leader reflects the society of which he or she is a part is given further provenance by the fact that it is generally recognised that Blair summed up the general mood of the nation when he reacted to the first news of the death of the Princess of Wales. It is not that he provided a lead; rather, being a consummate politician, he was able to articulate what people were feeling.

It is possible to make a solid case that it is much the same with business leaders. Those who – like John Major and his warm beer – pick on a facet of their community that is regarded as slightly odd or idiosyncractic risk ridicule. But those who are able to get to the nub of what makes people feel good about their organisation at a particular time can, like Ronald Reagan and his evocation of 'Morning in America', enjoy a good measure of success.

Since not even his most ardent supporters would suggest that Reagan was all-knowing, his example is a neat illustration of how leadership perhaps ought to be seen as a participative process. As Drath puts it, 'leadership is a dance'.

What is important about that realisation is that it 'opens up a new set of possibilities for the practice of leadership'. He is thinking especially of the idea that it should be a 'distributed function' rather than the province of a single formal leader. The fact that late 1990s industrial Britain seems to be finding it hard to find and hang on to traditional all-powerful chief executives adds fuel to the idea.

Something of the same sort of thinking is going on in the mind of Peter Wickens. A former executive of many corporations, most notably Nissan, he points out in the revised version of his 1995 book *The Ascendant Organisation* that, although much literature seems to 'suggest that leadership exists only at the very top', leaders in fact 'achieve results by working with and through people and can and should be present at all levels of the organisation'.

He says that most of the leaders given so much space in the business press and in books 'are creatures of their time and place' and while they may build or transform their organisations, they tend to have few transferable lessons. And if this alone is not enough to confound the consultants, he adds: 'Although the top leader is often vital to the success of the organisation, can set its tone and sometimes transform its values, such leaders, working alone, achieve nothing.'

Meanwhile, though, it is increasingly apparent that much of the rhetoric surrounding teamwork is empty. All the time that consultants, executives and academics are extolling the virtues of groups of people working together in co-operation, the literature concentrates on leaders. There is even a book that contains a series of chapters headed with the names of well-known chief executives credited with success or otherwise at their respective organisations.

Consequently, Wickens' message that everyone can exercise leadership seems especially important at a time when, at the same time as there is all the talk about delegation and the dreaded 'empowerment', middle managers are constantly finding themselves under the cosh. A 1998 announcement from British Steel, for example, makes clear that many of the thousands of jobs to go in the next part of the continuing effort to make the company more efficient will come from the ranks of middle managers.

As he says, most people are not able to become chief executives, 'but that does not mean that they cannot exercise leadership in the jobs they do'. As soon as a person has just one other to supervise, one process to influence or one facility to control, they can exercise leadership.

One of the troubles is, though, that leadership is too often associated with confrontation, especially in the UK and the USA. Wickens cites how Sir Neville Bowman-Shaw, former chairman and joint owner with his brother of the fork-lift truck maker Lancer Boss, reportedly behaved in an autocratic manner when the organisation bought a Spanish company – threatening the workers that if they messed things up, the factory would be closed. Nor was this apparently an exception. Labour turnover in the British factory was as high as 30 per cent at one point and works managers often left out of frustration, says Wickens. A few years later, German banks withdrew their support and the company became part of the German group Junghein-Rich – soon after which 'every possible performance indicator had improved dramatically, including labour turnover down to 8 per cent and absenteeism down to 3 per cent'.

This is not to say that there is never any place for confrontation. Wickens claims that Sir Michael Edwardes' readiness to take on the extremists at what was then still British Leyland paved the way for others to start to build the company later known as Rover Group. But he argues that simply concentrating on getting control back to management 'is no way to run a company'.

Instead, he quotes with approval Bill Hewlett as saying: 'What is the Hewlett-Packard way? I feel that in general terms it is the policies and actions that flow from the belief that men and women want to do a good job, a creative job, and that if they are provided with the proper environment, they will do so.'

He also describes how Jan Carlzon, president of Scandinavian Airlines, told Nissan managers in 1990 that 'the role of the leader will be that of a visionary, a strategic leader, who gives the objectives, who guides the way to reach those objectives'.

Though he stresses that there is no single model, he believes that there are certain 'behaviours and characteristics that can make for success in the ascendant organisation'. Personal attributes include general intelligence, empathy with people at all levels, the ability to act intuitively and be right most of the time, high levels of personal integrity and the drive to achieve, while a good leader's strategic perspective might include such aspects as a concern for all stakeholders, an ability to develop a vision based on this perspective rather than immediate issues and a willingness to challenge the status quo continuously.

The ability to communicate in all sorts of ways is also of great importance. But Wickens – who, incidentally, strays far beyond leadership in his description of the sort of approaches businesses must take to achieve sustainable, long-term success – says that 'perhaps the most important ability a leader can possess is having the wisdom and judgement to employ good people and give them headroom'.

> *'Perhaps the most important ability a leader can possess is having the wisdom and judgement to employ good people and give them headroom.' – management writer and former executive Peter Wickens.*

Some leaders, such as Virgin's Richard Branson and Nucor's Ken Iverson, already appear to realise this. But it is something that ego-heavy boardrooms around the world – and especially those in Britain, where notions of workplace democracy still appear alien – are going to have to ponder as their environment becomes more complex and their geographical spread wider.

Through their efforts to promote the efforts of their various lieutenants, such people are evidence of what could turn out to be a backlash against the idea of the all-seeing, all-knowing grand leader.

Indeed, research presented to the conference of the US Academy of Management in August 1998 indicates that, contrary to popular perceptions and much business reporting, strong

CEO personality traits alone have little connection to strong financial returns for the company. Even strong CEOs can have their efforts undone by dysfunctional senior management teams, says Randall Peterson of Cornell University's Johnson School of Management.

Echoing the views of leadership expert Warren Bennis in his book *Organizing Genius*, Peterson, a social psychologist who wrote the paper with Pamela Owens and Paul Martorana of the University of California at Berkeley's psychology department, claims that in successful companies the CEO fosters healthy group dynamics among his immediate subordinates, allowing them to mobilise the energies and talents throughout the organisation to overcome key problems and create new opportunities for growth. In particular, the study points out that successful top management teams had both a 'directive' leader and greater openness to new information.

'Disney's Michael Eisner and Coke's [the late] Roberto Goizueta had strong, consistent and clear visions for their companies, but they were also open to criticism and made successful adjustments when advised their case had altered', says Peterson.

He points out that there is a tendency either to overstate the role of the CEO as star or to say that the CEO hardly matters. But he adds that the findings 'suggest a synthesis of these factors, that the CEO's personality plays an important role when it is able to mesh with or foster similar strong values among his core group of lieutenants'.

Moreover, in the modern 'less hierarchical and more flattened organisation, having personality traits that enable you to manage and operate in teams will be essential for executives in profitable and growing companies', Peterson says.

The problem for British industry is that few organisations have yet to grasp the reality of working in this way. Most companies are alienating their workforces – those people they insist are their 'greatest asset' – and thus landing themselves with demotivated overheads rather than enthused partners.

The answer is not, as so many executives seem to think, to exhort employees to work ever harder as they put even more emphasis on productivity. Those things are likely to follow if organisations succeed in genuinely engaging their people.

And that demands paying attention to the principles set out above. Companies and other businesses that want to be successful in the new millennium are going to have to challenge the notion – which has reached its apogee in the USA – that just because technology has become so advanced work should be so dehumanised.

It is surely no coincidence that it is the USA that has seen the first attempts to develop a better balance between work and the rest of employees' lives. This is simply a predictable backlash against things going too far – of executives, clients and customers expecting too much of people. It is a little odd that after years of regarding substantial parts of continental Europe as rather backward for taking summer holidays and lunch breaks, Americans are calling into question their assumptions about the way business is conducted.

This is not before time because it is clear that a model that served its purpose well – even if it produced many casualties along the way – is unsustainable in an environment in which increasingly cynical, angry and frustrated employees are realising their importance and acknowledging that they do not have to put up with such a way of doing things.

Many people have already voted with their feet. One of the main reasons for the large-scale absence of women in Britain's boardrooms is that a lot of talented female managers take themselves out of the running for high office by setting up on their own – often with great success.

It seems clear that many British organisations are going to be left with just those workers who lack the spark to do anything else unless they can find a way of engaging those who would otherwise strike out on their own. A more open – and democratic – way of leading than British companies have been used to will be critical.

However, even more essential will be an acceptance of what might be termed 'the rules of engagement'. Only by following principles like those set out here can UK organisations hope to survive in a world made much smaller by the development of the single European currency, the growth of the Internet and rampant globalisation.

REFERENCES
AND FURTHER
READING

BOOKS

Scott Adams, *Build a Better Life By Stealing Office Supplies –
Dilbert's Big Book of Business* (Nicholas Brealey, 1992).

Scott Adams, *Clues for the Clueless – Dilbert's Big Book of
Manners* (Nicholas Brealey, 1993).

Scott Adams, *Still Pumped from Using the Mouse* (Boxtree,
1996).

Scott Adams, *I'm Not Anti-Business, I'm Anti-Idiot* (Boxtree,
1998).

Stephen Aris, *Arnold Weinstock and the Making of GE* (Au-
rum Press, 1998).

W.H. Auden, 'The Managers', in *Collected Poems* (Faber and
Faber, 1994).

Warren Bennis with Patricia Ward Biederman, *Organizing Genius: The Secrets of Creative Collaboration* (Nicholas Brealey, 1997).

Andrew Black, Philip Wright and John E. Bachman with John Davies, *In Search of Shareholder Value: Managing the Drivers of Performance* (FT Pitman, 1998).

Ashley Braganza and Andrew Myers, *Business Process Redesign: A View from the Inside* (International Thomson Business Press, 1998).

Alex Brummer and Roger Cowe, *Weinstock: The Life and Times of Britain's Premier Industrialist* (HarperCollins Business, 1998).

John Case, *The Open-Book Management Experience* (Nicholas Brealey, 1998).

Ben Cohen and Jerry Greenfield, *Ben & Jerry's Double-Dip: Lead With Your Values and Make Money Too* (Simon & Schuster, 1997).

James C. Collins and Jerry I. Porras, *Built to Last: Successful Habits of Visionary Companies* (Century, 1994).

Judith Crown and Glenn Coleman, *No Hands: The Rise and Fall of the Schwinn Bicycle Company, an American Institution* (Henry Holt and Company, 1996).

William Davis, *Great Myths of Business* (revised paperback edition, Kogan Page, 1998).

John Donovan, Richard Tully and Brent Wortman, *The Value Enterprise: Strategies for Building a Value-Based Organization* (McGraw-Hill Ryerson, 1998).

Tom Duncan and Sandra Moriarty, *Driving Brand Value: Using Integrated Marketing to Manage Profitable Stakeholder Relationships* (McGraw-Hill, 1997).

John Elkington, *Cannibals With Forks, The Triple Bottom Line of 21st Century Business* (Capstone, 1997).

Bob Garratt, *The Fish Rots From The Head: The Crisis In Our Boardrooms – Developing the Crucial Skills of the Competent Director* (HarperCollins Business, 1996).

Dwight L. Gertz and Joao P.A. Baptista, *Grow To Be Great: Breaking the Downsizing Cycle* (Simon & Schuster, 1995).

Arie de Geus, *The Living Company: Growth, Learning and Longevity in Business* (Nicholas Brealey, 1997).

Sumantra Ghoshal and Christopher A. Bartlett, *The Individualized Corporation: Great Companies Are Defined by Purpose, Process and People* (HarperCollins Business, 1997).

Adrian Gilpin, *Unstoppable People: How Ordinary People Achieve Extraordinary Things* (Century Business, 1998).

Rob Goffee and Gareth Jones, *The Character of a Corporation* (HarperCollins Business, 1998).

Mark Goyder, *Living Tomorrow's Company* (Gower, 1998).

Charles Hampden-Turner and Fons Trompenaars, *Mastering the Infinite Game: How East Asian Values are Transforming Business Practices* (Capstone, 1997).

Susannah Hart and John Murphy (eds), *Brands: The New Wealth Creators* (Macmillan Business, 1998).

Robert Heller, *The Naked Manager for the Nineties* (Little, Brown, 1995).

Peter Herriot, Wendy Hirsh and Peter Reilly, *Trust and Transition: Managing Today's Employment Relationship* (John Wiley & Sons, 1998.

Nicholas von Hoffman, *Capitalist Fools: Tales of American Business from Carnegie to Malcolm Forbes* (Chatto & Windus, 1993).

Frederick G. Hilmer and Lex Donaldson, *Management Redeemed: Debunking the Fads that Undermine our Corporations* (Simon & Schuster, 1997).

Ken Iverson with Tom Varian, *Plain Talk: Lessons from a Business Maverick* (John Wiley & Sons, 1998).

Robert Johansen and Rob Swigart, *Upsizing the Individual in the Downsized Organization; Managing in the Wake of Re-engineering, Globalization, and Overwhelming Technological Change* (Century, 1995).

Otto Kalthoff, Ikujiro Nonaka and Pedro Nueno, *The Light and The Shadow: How Breakthrough Innovation is Shaping European Business* (Capstone/Roland Berger Foundation, 1997).

Peter Kinder, Steven D. Lydenberg and Amy L. Domini, *Investing for Good: Making Money While Being Socially Responsible* (HarperCollins Business, 1994).

James AA Knight, *Value-Based Management: Developing a Systematic Approach to Creating Shareholder Value* (McGraw-Hill, 1997).

Simon Knox and Stan Maklan, *Competing on Value: bridging the gap between brand and customer value* (Financial Times Publishing, 1998).

George Labovitz and Victor Rosansky, *The Power of Alignment: How Great Companies Stay Centred and Accomplish Extraordinary Things* (John Wiley & Sons, 1997).

David H. Maister, *True Professionalism* (Simon & Schuster, 1997).

David H. Maister, *Managing the Professional Service Firm* (Simon & Schuster paperback, 1997).

David Matheson and Jim Matheson, *The Smart Organization: Creating Value through Strategic R&D* (Harvard Business School Press, 1998).

Malcolm McIntosh, Deborah Leipziger, Keith L. Jones and Gill Coleman, *Corporate Citizenship* (Financial Times Management, 1998).

Christopher Meyer, *Relentless Growth: How Silicon Valley Innovation Strategies Can Work In Your Business* (Simon & Schuster, 1997).

Barry J. Nalebuff and Adam M. Brandenburger, *Co-opetition* (HarperCollins Business, 1996).

Jeffrey Pfeffer, *The Human Equation, Building Profits by Putting People First* (Harvard Business School Press, 1997).

Price Waterhouse Financial & Cost Management Team, *CFO: Architect of the Corporation's Future* (John Wiley & Sons, 1997) .

James Brian Quinn, Jordan J. Baruch and Karen Anne Zien, *Innovation Explosion: Using Intellect and Software to Revolutionize Growth Strategies* (Simon & Schuster, 1997).

Alfred Rappaport, *Creating Shareholder Value* (revised edition Simon & Schuster, 1998).

Larry Reynolds, *The Trust Effect: Creating the High-Trust, High-Performance Organization* (Nicholas Brealey, 1997).

Jeffrey L. Rodengen, *The Legend of Nucor Corporation* (Official History of Nucor, Write Stuff Enterprises, 1997).

Hal F. Rosenbluth and Diane McFerrin Peters, *The Customer Comes Second and Other Secrets of Exceptional Service* (William Morrow & Co, 1992).

David Sadtler, Andrew Campbell and Richard Koch, *Break Up! When Large Companies are Worth More Dead than Alive* (Capstone, 1997).

Anthony Sampson, *Company Man, The Rise and Fall of Corporate Life* (HarperCollins, 1995).

Peter Schwartz, *The Art of the Long View: Planning for the Future in an Uncertain World* (John Wiley & Sons, 1996).

Mark Scott, *Value Drivers: The manager's framework for identifying the drivers of corporate value creation* (John Wiley & Sons, 1998).

Eileen C. Shapiro, *Fad Surfing in the Boardroom: Reclaiming the Courage to Manage in the Age of Instant Answers* (Capstone, 1997).

Eileen C. Shapiro, *The Seven Deadly Sins of Business: Freeing the Corporate Mind from Doom-Loop Thinking* (Capstone, 1998).

Howard Schultz and Dori Jones Yang, *Pour Your Heart Into It* (Hyperion, 1997).

Adrian J. Slywotzky and David J. Morison with Bob Andelman, *The Profit Zone: How Strategic Business Design Will Lead You to Tomorrow's Profits* (John Wiley & Sons, 1997).

Kevin Thomson, *Passion At Work* (Capstone, Oxford, 1998)

Peter D. Wickens, *The Ascendant Organisation* (revised edition, Macmillan Business, 1998).

Sloan Wilson, *The Man in the Grey Flannel Suit* (Cassell & Co, 1956).

Jerry Yoram Wind & Jeremy Main, *Driving Change: How the Best Companies Are Preparing for the 21st Century* (Kogan Page, 1998).

MAGAZINES AND JOURNALS

Stevan Alburty, 'The Ad Agency to End All Ad Agencies' (profile of St Luke's in *Fast Company*, December–January, 1997).

Bill Birchard, 'Hire Great People Fast' (article on recruitment practices of Cisco Systems and other Silicon Valley companies, *Fast Company*, August–September 1997).

Kerry A. Bunker, 'The Power of Vulnerability in Contemporary Leadership' (*Consulting Psychology Journal: Practice and Research*, Spring 1997).

Centre for Tomorrow's Company, *The Inclusive Approach and Business Success: The Research Evidence* (Gower, 1998).

Centre for Tomorrow's Company, *Sooner, Sharper, Simpler ... A lean vision of an inclusive Annual Report* (Gower, 1998).

Michael Chambers and Patrick Wilkins, 'Decline and Fall: The End of Frere Cholmeley Bischoff' (*Commercial Lawyer*, May 1998).

Confederation of British Industry, *1998 Innovation Trends Survey*.

Coopers & Lybrand, *The Innovation Survey* (1997).

Hugo Dixon, 'Poverty of ambition' (*Financial Times*, 21 August 1998).

Peter Drucker, 'The Theory of the Business' (*Harvard Business Review*, September–October 1994).

FDS International, 'Small & Medium Enterprises Silver Jubilee Survey Report' (1998).

Orit Gadiesh and James L. Gilbert, 'Profit Pools: A Fresh Look at Strategy', 'How to Map Your Industry's Profit Pool' (both *Harvard Business Review*, May–June 1998).

Sumantra Ghoshal and Donald Sull, 'Loss of faith in managers' (*Financial Times*, 6 June 1997).

Linda Grant, 'Monsanto's Bet: There's Gold in Going Green' (*Fortune*, 14 April 1997).

Rob Gray *et al.*, *The Valuation of Assets and Liabilities: Environmental Law and the Impact of the Environmental Agenda for Business* (The Institute of Chartered Accountants of Scotland, 1998).

Victoria Griffiths, 'A look into the soul of business' (*Financial Times*, 20 November 1997).

Gary Hamel, 'Strategy as Revolution' (*Harvard Business Review*, July-August 1996).

Gary Hamel, 'Strategy Innovation and the Quest for Value' (*Sloan Management Review*, Winter 1998).

Gary Hamel, 'Wrong merger, wrong logic' (*Financial Times*, 15 April 1998).

Ronald Henkoff, 'Growing Your Company: Five Ways to Do It Right' (*Fortune*, 25 November 1998).

John Holusha, 'Learning from the Turnaround at AK Steel', (*Strategy & Business*, Fourth Quarter 1997).

David M. Horth and Charles J. Palus, 'Learning to Lead Creatively' (*Strategy & Business*, Third Quarter 1996).

Institute of Management, 'A Green and Pleasant Land' (*Report on Managers' Views on Environmental Concerns*, May 1998).

Institute of Personnel and Development, *The People Management Implications of Leaner Ways of Working* (October 1996).

Kinsley Lord management consultants, 'Deliver the Dream' (paper, 1996).

Irvine Lapsley, Sue Llewellyn with Gavin Burnett, *Inside Hospital Trusts: Management Styles, Accounting Constraints* (The Institute of Chartered Accountants of Scotland, 1998).

Charles Leadbeater, 'A piece of the action: employee ownership, equity pay and the rise of the knowledge company' (Demos Paper no. 28, 1997).

Robert Lindsay, 'Freres: an offer it could not refuse' (Analysis of the causes of the demise of City law firm Frere Cholmeley Bischoff in *The Lawyer*, 12 May 1998) .

Arthur D. Little, *Global Survey on Innovation* (1998).

Charles E. Lucier and Amy Asin, 'Toward a New Theory of Growth' (*Strategy & Business*, Winter 1996).

Alex Markels, 'Power to the People' (profile of AES in *Fast Company*, February-March 1998).

Sarah Marks, 'Head in the Sand' (profile of Travers Smith Braithwaite in *Legal Business*, December–January 1997).

Sarah Marks, 'The Co-op, the thief, the banker and the lawyer' (analysis of Travers Smith Braithwaite role in bid for Co-operative Wholesale Society in *Legal Business*, June 1997).

Sarah Marks, 'Wilde Gamble' (analysis of planned Arthur Andersen/Wilde Sapte link-up in *Legal Business*, April 1998).

William M. Mercer Management Consultants, 'Transforming the HR Function for Global Business Success', (Report for The Conference Board).

Frank Morris, 'Why Business Needs An Intelligent Approach' (Cambridge Consultants house journal *Interface*, Winter 1997).

Nina Munk, 'Organisation Man' (Analysis of 'gold-collar workers' in *Fortune*, 16 March 1998).

Rob Norton, 'Exploding the Myths About Growth' (*Fortune*, 25 November 1996).

PA Consulting Group, *Managing for Shareholder Value* (1997).

PA Consulting Group, *The British Quality of Management Awards Report: An analysis of the 1997 survey and conclusions from a five year study of UK plcs* (1998).

Richard Pascale, 'Grassroots leadership' (article on Royal/Dutch Shell in *Fast Company*, April–May 1998).

Randall S. Peterson, Pamela Owens and Paul V. Martorana, 'Organizational Performance and CEO Personality: Explaining More of the Variance Through Top Management Team Group Dynamics' (Johnson Graduate School of Management, Cornell University, 1998).

Research International Observer, 'Connecting with the Baby Boomers' (May 1997).

'Responsible Business' (special supplement printed with *Financial Times*, May 1998).

Stephen Roach, 'America's recipe for industrial extinction' (*Financial Times*, 14 May 1996).

Anita Roddick, 'Commitment and Community' (Newell and Sorrell Utopian Paper no 7, September 1997).

Anthony J. Rucci, Steven P. Kirn and Richard T. Quinn, 'The Employee–Customer–Profit Chain at Sea' (*Harvard Business Review*, Januray–February 1998).

Thomas A Stewart, 'America's Most Admired Companies' (*Fortune*, 2 March 1998).

Thomas A. Stewart, 'Gray Flannel Suit?' (Examination on new 'organisation man' in *Fortune*, 16 March 1998).

Craig Vetter, 'He's Not Worthy' (Profile of Patagonia founder Yvon Chouinard in *Outside* magazine, January 1997).

Jeremy Warner, 'What happened to vision and ambition?' (Outlook, *The Independent*, 4 October 1997).

Richard Waters, 'A Return to Downsizing' (*Financial Times*, 6 October 1997).

WfD, 'The Great Work/Life Debate' (June 1998).

Chris Zook and Jimmy Allen, 'Strategies for Growth' (Bain & Co paper, 1998).

INDEX